Śrīmad Bhagavad Gītā

Chapter XI

The Text in Devanāgrī
with Transliteration in Roman letters,
Word-for-Word meaning in Text order with Translation
and
Commentary
by

Swami Chinmayananda

CENTRAL CHINMAYA MISSION TRUST
MUMBAI - 400 072.

Printed upto	December	1999	-	18000 copies
Reprint	November	2002	-	1000 copies
Reprint	May	2004	-	1000 copies
Reprint	December	2005	-	1000 copies
Reprint	July	2006	-	2000 copies

Published by:

CENTRAL CHINMAYA MISSION TRUST
Sandeepany Sadhanalaya
Saki Vihar Road,
Mumbai - 400 072, INDIA.
Tel: 91-22-28572367 / 28575806
Fax: 91-22-28573065
Email: ccmt@vsnl.com
Website: www.chinmayamission.com

Distribution Centre in USA:

CHINMAYA MISSION WEST
Publications Division,
560 Bridgetown Pike,
Langhorne, PA 19053, USA.
Tel: (215) 396-0390
Fax: (215) 396-9710
Email: publications@chinmaya.org
Website: www.chinmayapublications.org

Printed by

SAGAR UNLIMITED
28-B, Nand-Deep Industrial Estate,
Kondivita Lane, Andheri Kurla Road,
Mumbai-400 059.
Tel.: 28362777 / 28227699

Price: Rs. 30=00

ISBN 81-7597-093-6

Preface to the Revised Edition

After hearing the Lord say: "I am what manifests as the Self in all beings,... with an atom of My being, I pervade and sustain everything," *Arjuna* wanted to have a direct experience of the Divine Majesty, which is the source of support of all Existence.

To enable *Arjuna* to have a direct experience of the Divine, the Lord bestows upon him a new intuitive power of insight. Thereafter, the Lord reveals to him His cosmic form in which *Arjuna* finds, in an instant, all that exists—past, present and future—spread out, as it were, as part and parcel of an All-comprehending Whole, a Divine Person, whose mortifying majesty and stunning splendour are too much for him to bear. The Lord reveals that all beings are helplessly drawn and absorbed into His being—by the stringent Time, identified with the Lord Himself.

There is only Divine Will which encompasses the will of all beings, who are mere divine instruments serving His biddings and accomplishing His plans. *Arjuna* finds both the armies arrayed in battle formations, along with their warriors and Chiefs, have all been already destroyed by the Lord's Will; he, finding himself just an instrument of the Lord, surrenders to Him in dauntless devotion.

In this revised Edition diacritical marks are used for Transliteration of *Saṁskṛta* words in the verses as well as commentary. Non-English words have been italicised. In the 'free translation' section where the entire text is italicised, to distinguish *Saṁskṛta* words, 'normal' fonts are used. In the 'word-for-word meaning' section, for the benefit of readers not knowing *Devanāgarī,* transliteration of *Saṁskṛta* words is added. This will help readers to identify and pronounce the words correctly.

The English plural sign 's' has been added to untranslated *Saṁskṛta* words after a hyphen (-) to show that it is not elemental to the words e.g., *mantrā-s, Vedā-s, Ṛṣī-s* etc. Macrons are used on the last letter e.g., *'ā, ī'* of such words as *mantrā-s*, *Vedā-s*, *Ṛṣī-s* etc., to lengthen the quantity of sound to keep up with the prolonged sound in pronunciation, although grammer rules do not require so.

The commentary on *Gītā* (chapter-wise) has been reprinted repeatedly to meet continuous demand resulting in numerous inaccuracies, rendering some concepts almost unintelligible. Besides its readability was poor in small print. Both these aspects are taken care of in the revised layout, the credit for which is due to Shri Vishwamitra Puri who with consistent perseverance and devotion scrutinised the entire book very minutely to identify misprints, missing words and lines; added diacritical marks and word meanings, improved the get up; and pursued steadfastly, the suggested changes/ improvements, with the *Ācārya* of *Sāndīpany* Mumbai for approval.

An "Alphabetical Index" in *Devanāgarī* of the first line of verses, and "Glossary of Terms used," "Index to Topics," "the Essence of *Gītā,*" "Appellations of *Arjuna*" and "Names of *Śrī Kṛṣṇa*" are added to the volume containing Chapter-I of the present series. An "Alphabetical Index" in Roman letters, the beginning of first line in case of verses with two lines, and of first and third lines of verses having four lines is being appended at the end Chapter XVIII of the series. *Gītā* (chapter-wise) is being printed afresh in the revised format.

To be true to the *Saṁskṛta* text in transliteration, we have used "*brāhmaṇa*" for the first *Varṇa* instead of the commonly used word "*brahmin.*" It need not be confused with the term "*Brahman*" of the *Vedāntin*-s.

To facilitate easy location of a particular verse distinctive markings are given on the top of each page along with Chapter number and Name of the Chapter.

A key to the transliteration and pronunciation is added in the beginning of the book.

We are pleased to bring out the present revised Edition of the original commentary given by *H. H. Svāmī Chinmayānanda* whom we all reverentially refer as *Pūjya Gurudeva.* This is our humble offering at His holy feet with a prayer that may His words and guidance inspire us to carry on His work in all spheres of activities such as this---publication of scriptural thoughts for the benefit of the society.

Mahā Śivarātrī Day,
25th February, 1998. **Publishers**

TRANSLITERATION AND PRONUNCIATION GUIDE

ॐ	oṁ	h<u>ome</u>	ॐ	oṁ	R<u>ome</u>
अ	a	f<u>u</u>n	ट	ṭa	<u>t</u>ouch
आ	ā	c<u>a</u>r	ठ	ṭha	an<u>t-h</u>ill
इ	i	p<u>i</u>n	ड	ḍa	<u>d</u>uck
ई	ī	f<u>ee</u>t	ढ	ḍha	go<u>dh</u>ood
उ	u	p<u>u</u>t	ण	ṇa	thu<u>n</u>der
ऊ	ū	p<u>oo</u>l	त	ta	(close to) <u>th</u>ink
ऋ	ṛ	<u>r</u>ig	थ	tha	(close to) pa<u>th</u>etic
ॠ	ṝ	(long ṛ)	द	da	(close to) fa<u>th</u>er
ऌ	ḷ	*	ध	dha	(close to) brea<u>the hard</u>
ए	e	pl<u>ay</u>	न	na	<u>n</u>umb
ऐ	ai	h<u>igh</u>	प	pa	<u>p</u>urse
ओ	o	<u>o</u>ver	फ	pha	sap<u>ph</u>ire
औ	au	c<u>ow</u>	ब	ba	<u>b</u>ut
अं	aṁ	**	भ	bha	a<u>bh</u>or
अः	aḥ	***	म	ma	<u>m</u>other
क	ka	<u>k</u>ind	य	ya	<u>y</u>oung
ख	kha	blo<u>ck</u>head	र	ra	<u>r</u>un
ग	ga	<u>g</u>ate	ल	la	<u>l</u>uck
घ	gha	lo<u>g-h</u>ut	व	va	<u>v</u>irtue
ङ	ṅa	si<u>ng</u>	श	śa	<u>sh</u>ove
च	ca	<u>ch</u>unk	ष	ṣa	bu<u>sh</u>el
छ	cha	mat<u>ch</u>	स	sa	<u>s</u>ir
ज	ja	<u>j</u>ug	ह	ha	<u>h</u>ouse
झ	jha	he<u>dgeh</u>og	ळ	(Note 1)	(close to) wor<u>l</u>d
ञ	ña	bu<u>n</u>ch	क्ष	kṣa	work<u>sh</u>eet
त्र	tra	<u>thr</u>ee	ज्ञ	jña	*
ऽ	'	unpronounced अ (a)	ऽऽ	"	Unpronounced आ (ā)

Note 1: " ḷ " itself is sometimes used. * No English Equivalent.
** Nasalisation of the preceding vowel. *** Aspiration of preceding vowel.

CHAPTER XI

THE COSMIC—FORM DIVINE

Introduction

In the general scheme of developing the theme, Lord *Kṛṣṇa* had already explained His immanence (*Vibhūti*) in all subjects of the world. This expansion of Himself in all objects and beings, as a perceptible Divine Presence, is exhaustively explained in the previous chapter entitled '*Vibhūti Yoga*'—the Divine Glories.

Studying this chapter, keeping in view this scheme of development in the *Gītā*, we detect here that a perfectly modern and scientific method of investigation is employed. An intellectual enquiry seeks, first of all, to gather enough data to support a theory, and thereafter it demands an experimental demonstration of the same, without which, the theory cannot be established. If, in the previous chapter, therefore, the *Gītā* has supplied us with enough data to prove that the Self is the substratum for the multiple world, in this chapter, the attempt is to supply *Arjuna* with a practical demonstration that everything does exist only in the Self.

The declaration that the mud is the essence of all pots, is established only when we prove, not only that all pots have mud in them, but also that the mud always potentially contains all pots of all shapes and dimensions. To see the mud in every pot, one has only to train one's eyes to detect the mud as separate from the pot-shapes, but to see all pots in the mud, no doubt, the observer needs a special 'eye.' He needs a sufficient sense of detachment and a scholarly amount of imagination without which it is impossible for him to detect the world-of-pots in any sample of mud.

Similarly, as was described in the last chapter, to see the Self peeping through the windows of finite objects is relatively an easy task; but it is hard, indeed, for a mortal to cognise at once the entire Universe in one Reality, the Self. And yet, this is possible with the 'eye' of knowledge, which knows so well the art of discrimination, and which has developed in itself a sufficient sense of detachment, so that the observer can forget, for the moment, all his attachments, and view on, in a spirit of hushed expectancy and thrilled wonderment.

What exactly makes the things of the world exist separately from one another? My physical structure is certainly separated from the form and substance of the book that I am reading, or the chair in which I sit, or the table that is in front of me. I am separated from all others, and everyone of them is separate from everything else. Scientifically viewed, the factor that determines the physical existence of all things in the world is the same. And yet, we do not feel the oneness—they, being separated from each other, exist as individualised entities. What exactly are the factors that divide body from body, that separate object from object?

On a careful analysis, it will be quite clear to the thinker that it is the concept of space that divides the physical structures into independent islands. That which separates me from you, or me from my book, is the intervening space. Within my forearm, from the elbow to the wrist, there is certainly a sense of oneness, because, there is no intervening space present within the homogeneity of its entire length, while my fingers are separate, each being interleaved with space. If the concept of space is totally blotted out, it will be clear that all objects will immediately come together into a happy embrace, and will represent themselves as one congenial, homogeneous whole.

And, in this mass of things, there must be all the shapes and forms of all the things of this world at one and the same place and time. This is the concept of the Cosmic-Man; the vision of the world, when viewed by a mind in which the concept of time and space has been dried up! Though, not totally.

Supposing a toy-maker makes out of wax hundreds of forms of animals, birds and creatures, and stocks them in a cupboard. Viewed through its glass panes, no doubt, the monkey-doll is different from the cow-doll and both of them are separate from the baby-doll. On the shelf of the cupboard, the same toys are separated from each other by the intervening space. But suppose the doll-maker changes his mind and he decides to destroy the whole lot and to make out of the stuff something more profitable. The toy-maker squeezes them into one ball of wax. In this act, the maker of the dolls has eliminated the spaces that were there between the dolls, and in this bringing them together he created a huge ball-of-wax on the surface of which we could see the traces of almost all the dolls that were brought together: perhaps, the tail of the monkey, the face of the cow, the smile of the child, and the head of the dog!

Similarly, if *Kṛṣṇa* could dry up "the concept of space" in the mind of *Arjuna*, the Prince would be able to see the whole Universe as though on his own palm. However, here we find that *Arjuna*'s mind was given enough freedom to move about within the space-limit of *Kṛṣṇa*'s divine structure. Naturally, he sees in the *Kṛṣṇa*-form the entire Universe compressed and packed.

This concept of the Cosmic-Man, and the actual vision of it in the *Gītā*, satisfies the demand for demonstration in any age of intellectual self-assertion. Having seen the form, *Arjuna* gets completely converted both in his faith and in his understanding.

In this chapter, we find how the exquisite dramatist in *Vyāsa* has squeezed the *Saṁskṛta* language dry to feed the beauty of his literary masterpiece. Apart from the chosen words and the mellifluous phrases, every metrical dexterity is being employed here, as an effective strategy to heighten the dramatic situation and to paint clearly the emotions of wonderment, amazement, fear, reverence, devotion, etc., in *Arjuna*. Altogether, in the dignity of the concept, in the beauty of its diction, in the artistry of its depiction and in its inner stream of drama, this chapter has been rightly upheld by all as one of the highest philosophical poems in the world's treasure-house of Sacred Books.

ॐ

श्री परमात्मने नमः

अथैकादशोऽध्यायः

अर्जुन उवाच-

मदनुग्रहाय परमं गुह्यमध्यात्मसंज्ञितम् ।
यत्त्वयोक्तं वचस्तेन मोहोऽयं विगतो मम ॥ १ ॥

Arjuna Uvāca—
Madanu-grahāya paramaṁ guhya-madhyātma-saṁjñitam,
yattva-yoktaṁ vacas-tena moho-'yaṁ vigato mama.

मद्-अनुग्रहाय *mad-anugrahāya* = out of compassion towards me; परमम् *paramam* = the highest; गुह्यम् *guhyam* = the secret; अध्यात्म-संज्ञितम् *adhyātma-saṁjñitam* = concerning the Self or Spirit; यत् *yat* = which; त्वया *tvayā* = by you; उक्तम् *uktam* = spoken; वचः *vacaḥ* = word; तेन *tena* = by that; मोहः *mohaḥ* = delusion; अयम् *ayam* = this; विगतः *vigataḥ* = gone; मम *mama* = my.

Arjuna Said:

1. *By this word of the highest secret concerning the Self, which You have spoken out of compassion towards me, my delusion is gone.*

In this opening stanza, *Arjuna* expresses his complete satisfaction at the details regarding the glories of the Lord which were described in the previous chapter. *Arjuna* appreciated that so much labour was spent by *Kṛṣṇa* only to bless his disciple and bring him out of delusion. To realise the unity in the diversity is to get an inoculation against the sorrows of plurality. The deft pen of *Vyāsa* beautifully registers the effectiveness of the last chapter upon a sincere student when he makes *Arjuna* confess: "This, my delusion, is gone."

Removal of a delusion or a misunderstanding is not *in itself the acquisition of knowledge* of the Real. Removal of delusion is one aspect of the process of knowing the Truth. *Arjuna* must be rightly feeling that his delusion—his firm faith in the separativeness of names and forms—can no longer hold its ground when his intellect has been educated to look forward to, and detect the "presence" of the Divine in the very world of his perceptions. But at the same time, he has not gained any visible experience of the Unity in the diversity; he has no personal experience of the oneness of things and beings, although theoretically at least, his intellect has come to accept this inherent Oneness.

The *Pāṇḍava* Prince, *Arjuna*, realises that *Kṛṣṇa* has so elaborately explained the theme in the previous chapter only "out of compassion towards me" (*Mad-anugrahāya*). This reminds us of *Kṛṣṇa* using almost the same term (in X-11) when He explains how He, abiding in the hearts of his devotees, destroys all their inner darkness born out of ignorance.

Out of compassion for Arjuna, *what were the supremely profound words that were given out by the Lord? ... Listen:*

भवाप्ययौ हि भूतानां श्रुतौ विस्तरशो मया ।
त्वत्तः कमलपत्राक्ष माहात्म्यमपि चाव्ययम् ॥ २ ॥

Bhavāpyayau hi bhūtānāṁ śrutau vistaraśo mayā,
tvattaḥ kamala-patrākṣa māhātmya-mapi cāvyayam.

भवाप्ययौ *bhavāpyayau* = the origin and dissolution; हि *hi* = indeed; भूतानाम् *bhūtānām* = of beings; श्रुतौ *śrutau* = have been heard; विस्तरशः *vistaraśaḥ* = in detail; मया *mayā* = by me; त्वत्तः *tvattaḥ* = from you; कमल पत्र अक्ष *kamala patra akṣa* = O Lotus-eyed;

माहात्म्यम् *māhātmyam* = greatness; अपि *api* = also; च *ca* = and; अव्ययम् *avyayam* = inexhaustible.

2. *The origin and destruction of beings, verily, have been heard by me in detail from You, O Lotus-eyed* Kṛṣṇa, *and also Your inexhaustible greatness.*

It is natural, in a discussion between the teacher and the taught, that at the end of a difficult lesson, on approaching the teacher with his doubts, the student should first of all prove to him that he has sufficiently understood the theme of the discussion. This entitles the student to ask the teacher his doubts and get them cleared. Following this traditional method, *Arjuna* is trying to show *Kṛṣṇa* that he has completely understood the main theme of the last chapter. He has listened to *Kṛṣṇa* and understood the "*origin and dissolution of beings, and also Your inexhaustible greatness.*"

And yet, a doubt remains which can be removed only when his intellect is convinced by a confident knowledge arising out of an actually observed demonstration. The stanza is preparing to meet such a demand. When a student, who has proved to have understood the logic of discussion already carried out, asks a legitimate question, or enquires after the remedy for a possible obstacle, a true teacher must help him out of his troubles by all possible means. We shall observe here in this chapter that the great *Yogeśvara* (*Kṛṣṇa*), out of sheer kindness, even condescends to show *Arjuna* the form of the Cosmic-Man because the disciple has demanded that he must see it.

The demand of the disciple is described in the following verse:

एवमेतद्यथात्थ त्वमात्मानं परमेश्वर ।
द्रष्टुमिच्छामि ते रूपमैश्वरं पुरुषोत्तम ॥ ३ ॥

Evam-etad-yathāttha tvam-ātmānaṁ parameśvara,
draṣṭum-icchāmi te rūpa-maiśvaraṁ puruṣottama.

एवम् *evam* = thus; एतत् *etat* = this; यथा *yathā* = as; आत्थ *āttha* = has declared, described; त्वम् *tvam* = thou; आत्मानम् *ātmānam* = yourself; परमेश्वर *parameśvara* = O Supreme Lord; द्रष्टुम् *draṣṭum* = to see; इच्छामि *icchāmi* = (I) desire; ते *te* = your; रूपम् *rūpam* = form; ऐश्वरम् *aiśvaram* = sovereign; पुरुषोत्तम *puruṣottama* = O *Puruṣa* Supreme.

3. *(Now) O Supreme Lord! As you have thus described Yourself, I wish to see (actually) Your Form Divine,* O Puruṣottama.

Indicating by a familiar idiom in *Saṁskṛta*, "So be it" (*evam-etat*), *Arjuna* accepts the technical thesis that has been declared by the Lord. Intellectually, it has been satisfactorily proved that the Lord is immanent in all names and forms. Still the intellect awaits the baptism of a demonstration. Therefore *Arjuna* says, "*I desire to see Your Īśvara-form.*" He is *Īśvara* who in Himself, expresses omnipotence, infinite wisdom, strength, virtue, splendour and extreme dispassion; these are the six qualities that are described in our *Śāstrā-s* as forming the characteristic features of the God-principle.

This was the occasion on which *Krsna* decided to show to *Arjuna* that the *Lord is not only immanent* in all forms, but He is also the vehicle or receptacle in which all names and forms have their existence and play—*He is also transcendent.*

Though, with the enthusiasm of a fanatic believer in intellectualism, *Arjuna* demands a demonstration, he immediately realises that his audacity has, perhaps, crossed the frontiers of decency.

He is trying to smoothen his words out in the following stanza:

मन्यसे यदि तच्छक्यं मया द्रष्टुमिति प्रभो ।
योगेश्वर ततो मे त्वं दर्शयात्मानमव्ययम् ॥ ४ ॥

Manyase yadi tac-chakyaṁ mayā draṣṭum-iti prabho,
yogeśvara tato me tvaṁ darśayāt-mānam-avyayam.

मन्यसे *manyase* = you think; यदि *yadi* = if; तत् *tat* = that; शक्यम् *śakyam* = possible; मया *mayā* = by me; द्रष्टुम् *draṣṭum* = to see; इति *iti* = thus; प्रभो *prabho* = O Lord; योगेश्वर *yogeśvara* = O Lord of *Yogā-s*; ततः *tataḥ* = then; मे *me* = me; त्वम् *tvam* = you; दर्शय *darśaya* = show; आत्मानम् *ātmānam* = (Your) Self; अव्ययम् *avyayam* = imperishable.

4. *If you, O Lord, think it possible for me to see It, do You please, then, O Lord of* Yogā-s, *show me Your Imperishable Self-form.*

The demand in the previous stanza has been repeated here, with a dignified humility and pure reverence. In our ordinary life, in all our respectful appeals and humble petitions we use such phrases as: "If I may be permitted to say," "I shall be much obliged if," "I have the honour to submit," "If I may have the leave to say so," etc. The *Pāṇḍava* Prince, as a result of a second thought, as it were, smoothens his soldier-like abrupt language used in the previous stanza and says that the Lord's ***Immutable Universal Form*** may be shown to him—"*if You think it is possible to see it.*"

The modesty and reverence shown here are not expressions of a faked emotion for cheap fulfilment of desires. This is evident from the term he is using in addressing the Lord in the verse. In the first line we find *Kṛṣṇa* being addressed as "O Lord" (*Prabho*), and in the following line He is again addressed as "the Lord of *Yogā-s*" (*Yogeśvara*). These clearly indicate that *Arjuna* has come to feel that *Kṛṣṇa* is not a mere mortal teacher, capable of giving only some intellectual ventilations and spiritual discourses, but that "He is Himself Divine and a Master-of-*Yoga*," and therefore, he is capable of fulfilling the request, if the "teacher" in *Kṛṣṇa* is satisfied that the "student" in *Arjuna* will be benefited by such a demonstration.

The humble request of an earnest student never falls on deaf ears, if it is made to a true teacher:

श्रीभगवानुवाच-

पश्य मे पार्थ रूपाणि शतशोऽथ सहस्रशः ।
नानाविधानि दिव्यानि नानावर्णाकृतीनि च ॥ ५ ॥

Śrī Bhagavān Uvāca—

Paśya me pārtha rūpāṇi śataśo-'tha sahasraśaḥ,
nānā-vidhāni divyāni nānā-varṇā-kṛtīni ca.

पश्य *paśya* = behold; मे *me* = my; पार्थ *pārtha* = O *Pārtha;* रूपाणि *rūpāṇi* = forms; शतशः *śataśaḥ* = by hundreds; अथ *atha* = and; सहस्रशः *sahasraśaḥ* = by thousands; नाना-विधानि *nānā-vidhāni*= of different sorts; दिव्यानि *divyāni* = divine; नाना-वर्ण-आकृतीनि *nānā-varṇa-ākṛtīni* = of various colours and shapes; च *ca* = and.

The Blessed Lord said:

5. *Behold,* O Pārtha, *My forms, by hundreds and thousands, of different sorts and Divine of various colours and shapes.*

If gold is the essential stuff in all the ornaments, every ornament in the world must be available in the total gold. To see the gold in the ornaments is relatively easy, it being a *physical perception.* But to detect the presence of all ornaments of different shapes and colours in the total gold is comparatively difficult, inasmuch as it is the *Vision of the intellect.*

Keeping this idea in mind, when you read the opening lines of the Lord's words, it becomes strikingly significant. "*Behold, My forms by hundreds and thousands, of different sorts and Divine of various colours and shapes.*" It was not necessary for *Kṛṣṇa* to change His form to that of the Cosmic-Man; all that *Arjuna* had to do was to *behold the form* right in front of him. But, unfortunately, the instrument-of-perception was not tuned up for the object of his investigation, and therefore, *Arjuna* could not perceive that which was already in *Kṛṣṇa.*

That which is lying beyond the focal length of a telescope, cannot be viewed by the observer even though the object may be present in line with the axis of the instrument. In order to bring the farther object within the span of vision, the observer will have to make the required adjustments in the telescope. Similarly, *Kṛṣṇa* did not *transform* Himself into His Cosmic-Form, but He only helped *Arjuna* to make the necessary inward adjustments so that he could perceive what was there evidently in *Kṛṣṇa.* Naturally, the Lord says, "*behold.*" The total world of perceivable beings of all shapes and colours is indicated in the enumeration made by the Lord in the stanza.

What are those?

पश्यादित्यान्वसून्रुद्रानश्विनौ मरुतस्तथा ।
बहून्यदृष्टपूर्वाणि पश्याश्चर्याणि भारत ॥ ६ ॥

paśyādityān-vasūn-rudrāna-śvinau marutas-tathā,
bahūnya-dṛṣṭa-pūrvāṇi paśyāś-caryāṇi bhārata.

पश्य *paśya* = behold; आदित्यान् *ādityān* = the *Ādityā-s* (the twelve sons of *Aditi*); वसून् *vasūn* = the (eight) *Vasū-s*; रुद्रान् *rudrān* = the (eleven) *Rudrā-s*; अश्विनौ *aśvinau* = the (two) *Aśvin-s*; मरुत: *marutaḥ* = the *Maruta-s* (fortynine types of winds including lightning, thunder, storms etc.); तथा *tathā* = also; बहूनि *bahūni* = many; अदृष्ट-पूर्वाणि *adṛṣṭa-pūrvāṇi* = never seen before; पश्य *paśya* = see; आश्चर्याणि *āścaryāṇi* = wonders; भारत *bhārata* = *O Bhārata.*

6. *Behold the* Ādityā-s, *the* Vasū-s, *the* Rudrā-s, *the (two)* Aśvin-s *and also the* Maruta-s; *behold many wonders never seen before,* O Bhārata.

In enumerating the items that are to be seen in *Kṛṣṇa*'s Cosmic-Form, the Lord hints at the most important and striking ones of them. This is generally done when we try to describe a crowd of people or things by using a short representative term. Mention is made on all such occasions of the most important items or personalities—the few who represent the whole crowd.

With a note of despair ringing through his words, the Lord concludes "*Behold many more such wonders as never seen before.*" The various items enumerated have all been already explained in the previous chapter.* Of them the only new term used here is the *Aśvini Kumārā-s*, the Horsemen-Twins. It is not very clear in literature as to what exactly is the identity of these twins with heads of horses. It is not very easy to decide what they represent. In some places they are described as the Dawn and the Dusk, and in other places there are sufficient evidences to make us suspect that they represent the Morning-Star and the Evening-Star. Anyway, they are Angels that go to serve their devotees in times of utter need and despair.

By giving a comprehensive summary of the things to be expected in the cosmic-vision, Kṛṣṇa *has increased the intellectual curiosity of his disciple. Where exactly is he to look for these things? ... Listen:*

इहैकस्थं जगत्कृत्स्नं पश्याद्य सचराचरम् ।
मम देहे गुडाकेश यच्चान्यद् द्रष्टुमिच्छसि ॥ ७ ॥

Ihai-kastham jagat-kṛtsnaṁ paśyādya sacarā-caram,
mama dehe guḍākeśa yac-cānyad draṣṭu-micchasi.

इह *iha* = in this, here; एकस्थम् *ekastham* = concentrated, centred in one; जगत् *jagat* = the universe; कृत्स्नम् *kṛtsnam* = whole; पश्य *paśya*

* The *Ādityā-s* and *Maruta-s* (X-21) *Gītā;* the *Vasū-s* and *Rudrā-s* (X-23) *Gītā.*

= behold; अद्य *adya* = now; सचर-अचरम् *sacara-acaram* = with the moving and unmoving; मम *mama* = my; देहे *dehe* = in body; गुडाकेश *guḍākeśa* = O *Guḍākeśa*; यत् *yat* = that; च *ca* = and; अन्यत् *anyat* = other; द्रष्टुम् *draṣṭum* = to see; इच्छसि *icchasi* = (you) desire.

7. *Now behold,* O Guḍākeśa, *in this Body, that the whole universe centred in One—including the moving and the unmoving—and whatever else you desire to see.*

The enthusiastic seeker's adventurous mind having been sufficiently educated so far to develop an unending wealth of 'eagerness to know,' *Kṛṣṇa* further educates, sharpening in the student, the 'anxiety to know' in this mind, with sufficient details on what he may expect in the Divine Vision that is to follow. This secret technique then makes the student ardently converge all his attention towards one given Form Divine. This is achieved by this verse. If we follow the technique, developed through the expressed words, we shall find that *Vyāsa* has here explained the entire Science of Love as adumbrated in the Cult of *Bhakti*, or 'Devotion to the Supreme.'

The entire Universe, constituted both of the moving and the unmoving—of the sentient and the insentient—is being shown by *Kṛṣṇa* on his own physical structure as described by the effective intimate term, "Here, concentrated" (*Iha-eka-stham*). And this term has been annotated in the same stanza as "In this, My Body" (*mama dehe*). The entire Universe of gross forms, both movable and immovable, is to be compressed within the framework of *Kṛṣṇa*'s girth and height. As we explained earlier* the concept of space has not been completely sponged out of *Arjuna*'s mind but a total space-concept equivalent to *Kṛṣṇa*'s own mortal dimensions is left in him. With this mind, when *Arjuna* looks out, he must necessarily see framed in *Kṛṣṇa* all at once, the entire Universe compressed and miniatured with all its multiple details intact.

* *Gītā* Ch. XI—Introduction.

Even though "the entire Universe, including both the moving and the unmoving" is a term sufficiently elastic so as not to leave anything outside its implications, *Kṛṣṇa* again sharpens the enthusiasm of *Arjuna* by stating that the *Pāṇḍava* could see anything *"else that you desire to see."* As a typical mortal, *Arjuna* is pre-occupied with the particular problem of life and his anxiety naturally grows to peep into the future and discover its solution rather than to realise the underlying oneness that embraces even the forms in the outer world-of-*matter*.

"The one in the many" has been described in the last chapter, and here we are about to see "the many in the one."

न तु मां शक्यसे द्रष्टुमनेनैव स्वचक्षुषा ।
दिव्यं ददामि ते चक्षुः पश्य मे योगमैश्वरम् ॥ ८ ॥

Na tu māṁ śakyase draṣṭum-anenaiva sva-cakṣuṣā,
divyaṁ dadāmi te cakṣuḥ paśya me yoga-maiśvaram.

न *na* = not; तु *tu* = but; माम् *mām* = me; शक्यसे *śakyase* = you can; द्रष्टुम् *draṣṭum* = to see; अनेन *anena* = with this; एव *eva* = even; स्वचक्षुषा *sva-cakṣuṣā* = with own eyes; दिव्यम् *divyam* = divine; ददामि *dadāmi* = (I) give; ते *te* = (to) you; चक्षुः *cakṣuḥ* = the eye; पश्य *paśya* = behold; मे *me* = my; योगम् *yogam* = *Yoga*; ऐश्वरम् *aiśvaram* = lordly.

8. *But you are not able to behold Me with these your own eyes; I give you the divine-eye; behold My lordly* Yoga.

We have already explained how it is relatively easy to see the essential stuff as the core of individual names and forms, but the reverse of it—to discover the many in the one—is the work of a subtle intellect functioning through right philosophical understanding. To *read* a poem, only a knowledge of the alphabet is necessary; but to *understand* its subtler beauties and to classify it in a comparative study with other similar poems, it needs a masterly mind that has been well soaked with the master-pieces in poetry. Similarly, to see "*the one in the many*" is the work of a 'heart' soaked with faith; but to *perceive* "*the many in the one*," we need, besides the 'heart,' an educated 'intellect' that has learnt to see for itself the logic of the philosophers. This peculiar capacity of an educated intellect to see the extra-ordinary is the *vision of the intellect* which is gained when we develop the *faculty to perceive* and *to know*.

This obvious fact is explained by the Lord in this stanza, "*you cannot see me with these eyes of yours; I give thee the vision divine*." There are very many critics who try to explain this "Divine-eye" through fantastic suppositions and ridiculous theories. Such commentators are certainly men, not much educated in the style of the *Hindū* scriptures, the *Upaniṣad-s*. Expressly and tacitly, all through the *Upaniṣad-s*, it is repeatedly explained that the subtler cannot be brought within the scope and compass of the instruments-of-perception given to man. The external sense organs can play freely only in the outer world-of-objects. Even when we ordinarily "see an idea" it is not done with our outer pair of eyes. The intellectual comprehension is meant here by the term "seeing" and the capacity of the intellect to comprehend is the 'Divine-eye.'

This "special-vision" is given to the *Pāṇḍava* Prince so that he may see "*My supreme Yoga-power*" by which the whole Universe of multiplicity is being supported by the Lord's own form. Earlier, this particular *Yoga*-Power of the Lord, has been already described at two different places (VII-12 and IX-4), almost in identical terms.

The scene shifts to Hastināpura, *in the palace of* Dhṛtarāṣṭra:

सञ्जय उवाच-

एवमुक्त्वा ततो राजन्महायोगेश्वरो हरिः ।
दर्शयामास पार्थाय परमं रूपमैश्वरम् ॥ ९ ॥

Sañjaya Uvāca—

Evam-uktvā tato rājan-mahā-yogeśvaro hariḥ,
darśayāmāsa pārthāya paramaṁ rūpa-maiśvaram.

एवम् *evam* = thus; उक्त्वा *uktvā* = having spoken; ततः *tataḥ* = then; राजन् *rājan* = O King; महा-योगेश्वरः *mahā-yogeśvaraḥ* = the great Lord of *Yoga*; हरिः *hariḥ* = *Hari*; दर्शयामास *darśayāmāsa* = showed; पार्थाय *pārthāya* = to *Pārtha*; परमम् *paramam* = supreme; रूपम् *rūpam* = form; ऐश्वरम् *aiśvaram* = lordly, sovereign.

Sañjaya said :

9. *Having thus spoken, O King, the great Lord of* Yoga, Hari, *showed to* Pārtha *His Supreme Form, as the Lord (of the Universe).*

The versatile genius of *Vyāsa* has never left anything that he has touched without raising it to the most sublime heights of perfection. With unimaginable capacities for composing incomparable poetry, unique prose-diction, chaste descriptions, artistic literary designs, original innovations both in thought and form—a brilliant philosopher, a man of consummate wisdom, a genius in worldly knowledge, at one time in the palace, at another time in the battle-field, at still another time in *Badrīnātha*, and again, among the silent snow peaks—strode the colossus, *Śrī Vyāsa*, as an embodiment of what is best in the *Hindū* tradition and in the *Āryan* culture. Such an all-round genius has not yet been reported ever to have been born, lived or achieved so much in the history of this globe, at any other time!

When such a mighty Master takes up his pen to paint life in all its implications and indicate an answer to all the eternal problems of man, he cannot but use the medium of drama in his work. Though the *Saṁskṛta* "*drama*," as is now known to us, is of a much later development, the dramatic interest has been fully and exhaustively exploited by the *Vyāsa*'s pen all through his works. A beautiful example of his dexterity as a dramatist is amply evident in this chapter, where the three personalities *Kṛṣṇa*, *Arjuna* and *Sañjaya*—together swing their audience of readers between the noisy battle-field of *Kurukṣetra* and the chambers of *Dhṛtarāṣṭra's* palace, where a hushed silence of impending tragedy thickly hung.

After Lord *Kṛṣṇa* gave *Arjuna* a hint as to what he should expect and where he would gain the vision of the Cosmic-Man, etc., *Vyāsa* introduces a small section in which *Sañjaya* reports to *Dhṛtarāṣṭra,* the blind father of the wicked *Kauravā-s.*

The literary purpose served by this stanza is only to show to the readers that *Kṛṣṇa*, according to his promise, had actually revealed his Cosmic-Form to *Arjuna.* But along with that, the deft mastery of the ancient writer of *Mahābhārata* tries to paint for us the mental attitude and the inward sympathies of *Sañjaya.* We have stated earlier that *Sañjaya* is "*Our own special correspondent.*" His sympathies are clearly with the *Pāṇḍavā*-s, the friends of the Lord. This tendency in *Sañjaya* is unquestionably revealed when he addressed his own Master merely as "O King" (*Rājan*) while he uses the terms, (a) *Mahāyogeśvara* ... "the Great Lord of *Yoga*" and (b) *Hariḥ* ... "the one who maintains the champions of Truth by destroying the powers of falsehood," to indicate Lord *Kṛṣṇa.* The implied suggestions of these words point at a bloodless murder of the blind old King!

With *Sañjaya*'s words, the crowd of listeners and students of *Gītā* are shifted from the field of the battle to the palace of the battle-monger. This is perhaps necessary to remind the readers that the philosophy of the *Gītā* has an intimate practical application to life. *Sañjaya* informs *Dhṛtarāṣṭra* that the Great Lord of *Yoga* showed to *Arjuna* his Supreme *Īśvara*-form. *Sañjaya* entertains a thin hope that, at least on hearing that the Lord of the Universe is on the side of his nephews, the blind King will foresee the sure defeat of his sons and, in his discrimination, will cry a halt to the impending disastrous war.

In a rough outline Sañjaya *describes the list of things that were visible within the framework of the divine charioteer:*

अनेकवक्त्रनयनमनेकाद्भुतदर्शनम् ।
अनेकदिव्याभरणं दिव्यानेकोद्यतायुधम् ॥ १० ॥

Aneka-vaktra-nayanam-anekād-bhuta-darśanam,
aneka-divyā-bharaṇaṁ divyā-neko-dyatā-yudham.

अनेक वक्त्र नयनम् *aneka vaktra nayanam* = with numerous mouths and eyes; अनेक-अद्भुत-दर्शनम् *aneka-adbhuta-darśanam* = with numerous wonderful sights; अनेक-दिव्य-आभरणम् *aneka-divya-ābharaṇam* = with numerous divine ornaments; दिव्य अनेक उद्यत-आयुधम् *divya-aneka-udyata-āyudham* = with numerous divine weapons uplifted.

10. With numerous mouths and eyes, with numerous wonderful sights, with numerous divine ornaments, with numerous divine weapons uplifted ... (such a form He showed.)

दिव्यमाल्याम्बरधरं दिव्यगन्धानुलेपनम् ।
सर्वाश्चर्यमयं देवमनन्तं विश्वतोमुखम् ॥ ११ ॥

Divya-mālyāmbara-dharaṁ divya-gandhānu-lepanam,
sarvāścarya-mayaṁ deva-manantaṁ viśvato-mukham.

दिव्य-माल्य-अम्बर-धरम् *divya-mālya-ambara-dharam* = wearing divine garlands (necklaces) and apparels; दिव्य-गन्ध-अनुलेपनम् *divya-gandha-anulepanam* = anointed with divine unguents (ointments or perfumes); सर्व-आश्चर्य-मयम् *sarva-āścarya-mayam* = the all-wonderful; देवम् *devam* = resplendent; अनन्तम् *anantam* = boundless; विश्वत: मुखम् *viśvataḥ mukham* = with faces on all sides.

11. Wearing divine garlands (necklaces) and apparels, anointed with divine unguents (perfumes), the all-wonderful, resplendent, boundless with faces on all sides.

When a painter at his easel tries to express his artistic ideas through the medium of colour, he invariably begins by outlining his theme roughly on the canvas. Later on, inch by inch, he adds more and more details to make the canvas sing the song of his message. Similarly in the word-picture of the literary artist, *Vyāsa,* this stanza containing *Sañjaya*'s words, represents the rough outline of the Universal Form of the Lord.

"Many many mouths and eyes"—"Numerous wonderful sights"—"of endless divine ornaments"—"with an artillery of celestial weapons uplifted" all these phrases represent the so many moulds into which the poetry of *Vyāsa* is poured and *Kṛṣṇa* the Universal Soul comes out carved in His Cosmic Form.

The Vision appearing before *Sañjaya* is no vision for a mortal intellect to live comfortably by. An ordinary man must feel dazed with wonderment and fear at this august and mighty Vision. The total Cosmos is no easy subject-matter for the mind to conceive of or for the intellect to comprehend, and therefore, when it comes as it does in the *Gītā*, in the stark realism of the Vision, *Sañjaya* stammers these phrases.

"Wearing divine garlands and apparels"—"anointed with divine unguents (perfumes)"—"All wonderful, the boundless, resplendent, with faces on all sides"—these represent the remaining strokes which, when added to the previous set of lines, bring out the picture of the Cosmic-Man roughly in its full outline.

Continuing in his language of dots and dashes, Sañjaya *describes:*

दिवि सूर्यसहस्रस्य भवेद्युगपदुत्थिता ।
यदि भाः सदृशी सा स्याद्भासस्तस्य महात्मनः ॥ १२ ॥

Divi sūrya-sahasrasya bhaved-yugapad-utthitā,
yadi bhāḥ sadṛśī sā syād-bhāsas-tasya mahātmanaḥ.

दिवि *divi* = in the sky; सूर्य सहस्रस्य *sūrya sahasrasya* = of a thousand suns; भवेत् *bhavet* = were; युगपत् *yugapat* = at once (simultaneously); उत्थिता *utthitā* = arisen; यदि *yadi* = if; भा: *bhāḥ* = splendour; सदृशी *sadṛśī* = like; सा *sā* = that; स्यात् *syāt* = would be; भास: *bhāsaḥ* = splendour; तस्य *tasya* = of that; महात्मन: *mahātmanaḥ* = of the mighty Being (great soul).

12. *If the splendour of a thousand Suns was to blaze all at once (simultaneously) in the sky, that would be like the splendour of that Mighty Being (great soul).*

After giving this hasty sketch of the Total-Form to the blind King, *Dhṛtarāṣṭra*, *Sañjaya* explains to him the glory of the Mighty One. The Lord, in His Universal-aspect, was dazzling in His own brilliance and the divine glory of it was almost blinding; and this may be another reason why more intimate details are not given by *Sañjaya* in the previous two verses. In order to convey this idea, *Sañjaya* is using this strange, but powerful, simile.

The glorious shine of that Mighty Being is almost, it is said, as luminous as that of a thousand Suns if they were to rise up all at once in the sky. In the *Upaniṣadik* lore also, we have the description of the *Ātman* almost in the same language. But somehow or other, it must be admitted that in the mouth of *Sañjaya*, especially when he is describing the Divine-Form of *Kṛṣṇa*, it gathers a new glamour and glory.

Beautifying the picture with some more details, Sañjaya *adds:*

तत्रैकस्थं जगत्कृत्स्नं प्रविभक्तमनेकधा ।
अपश्यद् देवदेवस्य शरीरे पाण्डवस्तदा ॥ १३ ॥

Tatraika-sthaṁ jagat-kṛtsnaṁ pravi-bhakta-manekadhā,
apaśyad deva-devasya śarīre pāṇḍavas-tadā.

तत्र *tatra* = there; एकस्थम् *ekastham* = resting in one; जगत् *jagat* = the universe; कृत्स्नम् *kṛtsnam* = the whole; प्रविभक्तम् *pravibhaktam* = divided; अनेकधा *anekadhā* = in many groups; अपश्यत् *apaśyat* = saw; देव देवस्य *deva devasya* = of the God of gods; शरीरे *śarīre* = in the body; पाण्डव: *pāṇḍavaḥ* = Son of *Paṇḍu*; तदा *tadā* = then.

13. *There, in the body of the God of gods, the* Pāṇḍava *(Son of* Paṇḍu*) then saw the whole Universe resting in one, with all its infinite parts.*

In that Divine Form of the Lord, *Arjuna* perceived how the entire world of manifold varieties had been brought together and packed to rest at one and the same place. We have already noticed that the concept of the Cosmic-Man is the vision of the Universe through a mind which has ceased to act with the concept of time or space. This vision of "*the many in one*" is not so much a physical perception as an intellectual comprehension. It is not that the Universe has shrunk into the size of *Kṛṣṇa.* It is quite sufficient if *Arjuna* has the required sense of oneness in the world of *matter* and if he looks at the Universe through his understanding so that, intellectually, he can come to estimate the oneness of the Universe.

To quote a parallel in modern science, we may consider the attempt of Chemistry to classify all the existing substances. When so many things in the world are brought on the laboratory tables, it is found that they are constituted of the elements, in all about one hundred and three in number. This understanding of the elements soon yields place when the atom-contents in them are discovered to be nothing other than the electrons, protons and neutrons. If a scientist, who knows these three were to look through his knowledge, at the manifold substances, it would be very easy for him to see that all things of the world are in these three factors, which are the contents of each atom. If fact now there are only three elements in the world, the triple factors in the Atom. Similarly here, when *Arjuna* gained his special knowledge through the grace of *Krṣna*, he comes to recognise the whole Universe in the very body of the God-principle, the Total-intellect.

Arjuna's *psychological and physical reactions on seeing this form, are being very carefully noted and reported by* Sañjaya:

ततः स विस्मयाविष्टो हृष्टरोमा धनञ्जयः ।
प्रणम्य शिरसा देवं कृताञ्जलिरभाषत ॥ १४ ॥

Tataḥ sa vismayā-viṣṭo hṛṣṭa-romā dhanañjayaḥ,
praṇamya śirasā devaṁ kṛtāñjalira-bhāṣata.

ततः *tataḥ* = then; सः *saḥ* = he; विस्मय-आविष्टः *vismaya-āviṣṭaḥ* = filled with wonder; हृष्टरोमा *hṛṣṭaromā* = with hair standing on end; धनञ्जय *dhanañjaya* = *Arjuna*; प्रणम्य *praṇamya* = having prostrated; शिरसा *śirasā* = with (his) head; देवम् *devam* = the God; कृताञ्जलिः *kṛtāñjaliḥ* = with joined palms; अभाषत *abhāṣata* = spoke.

14. *Then,* Dhanañjaya, *filled with wonder, with his hair standing on end, bowed down his head to the God and spoke with joined palms.*

On seeing this transcendental vision, emotions of wonderment and consequent horripilations are noticed in *Arjuna.* Though *Sañjaya* is far away, he not only seems to see minute physical details of each soldier upon the battle-field but also seems to have a power to peep over the body into the mind-and-intellect equipment of each individual. The inner wonder-emotion in *Arjuna*'s mind is as much evident to *Sañjaya*, as was his hair standing on his body. *Arjuna*, with folded palms, bending his head low, now opens his mouth for the first time to talk. That *Arjuna* did not speak so long is in itself a positive indication of the choking emotion that he must have felt at the sight of this sweetly unnerving Divine-Form.

What were the actual words of wonderment that burst out from Arjuna?—*Listen:*

अर्जुन उवाच-

पश्यामि देवांस्तव देव देहे
सर्वांस्तथा भूतविशेषसंघान् ।
ब्रह्माणमीशं कमलासनस्थम्
ऋषींश्च सर्वानुरगांश्च दिव्यान् ॥ १५ ॥

Arjuna Uvāca—

Paśyāmi devāṁs-tava deva dehe
sarvāṁs-tathā bhūta-viśeṣa-saṁghān,
brahmāṇa-mīśaṁ kamal-āsana-stham
ṛṣīṁś-ca sarvān-uragāṁś-ca divyān.

पश्यामि *paśyāmi* = (I) see; देवान् *devān* = the gods; तव *tava* = your; देव *deva* = O God; देहे *dehe* = in the body; सर्वान् *sarvān* = all; तथा *tathā* = also; भूत-विशेष-संघान् *bhūta-viśeṣa-saṁghān* = hosts of various classes of beings; ब्रह्माणम् *brahmāṇam* = *Brahmā*; ईशम् *īśam* = the Lord; कमल-आसन-स्थम् *kamala-āsana-stham* = seated on a Lotus; ऋषीन् *ṛṣīn* = Sages; च *ca* = and; सर्वान् *sarvan* = all; उरगान् *uragān* = serpents; च *ca* = and; दिव्यान् *divyān* = divine.

Arjuna said:

15. *I see all the gods, O God, in Your body, and (also) hosts of various classes of beings,* Brahmā, *the Lord of Creation, seated on a Lotus, all the* Ṛṣī-s *and celestial serpents.*

When the Prince addressed *Kṛṣṇa* as the Resplendent (*Deva*), he is endorsing the comparison of the Lord to the light of thousand-suns which was used earlier by *Sañjaya*. Enumerating the features recognised by him on the body of *Kṛṣṇa*, *Arjuna* says, "*In thy body I see all the devā-s and hosts of all grades of beings.*" This was already indicated by *Sañjaya* when he described the Universal Form as '*wearing numerous robes*,' '*adoring itself with different types of divine ornaments*,' '*wearing garlands of celestial beauty*,' and bearing '*an arsenal of weapons in Its innumberable hands*.'

These descriptions show that in *Kṛṣṇa* one could recognise not only the things of the world, but in the *Virāṭ*-form of the Lord even the *Devā-s* are represented. The same *ādhidaiva*-idea is very directly insisted upon by *Arjuna* in this stanza when he describes among the things that he saw in *Kṛṣṇa*, the Creator, *Brahmājī* (*Brahmāṇam*), the Annihilator, *Śiva* (*Īśam*), and the Sustainer, *Viṣṇu* (*Kamal-āsana-stham*); along with a host of ancient *Seers*!

And celestial serpents:—In poetry, it is a technique, often very effective, employed by great poets wherein they suddenly step down from the sublime to the ridiculous or the grotesque, only to shock the readers and thereby tap out of them the degree of special attention which the theme demands. It is indicated here that from *Brahmājī* in the heavens, to the serpents in the holes of the earth, all are represented in the Lord's Cosmic-Form. The microcosm (*Vyaṣṭi*) is the macrocosm (*Samaṣṭi*). And this is explained and realised by all great thinkers of the world. But no body has ever before tried to express this philosophical idea in the form of a vivid objective representation. *Vyāsa* was the pioneer in this art and none has yet dared to follow him in this arduous task.

The gripping details that can unnerve even the most courageous are given out now by Arjuna*:*

अनेकबाहूदरवक्त्रनेत्रं
पश्यामि त्वां सर्वतोऽनन्तरूपम् ।
नान्तं न मध्यं न पुनस्तवादिं
पश्यामि विश्वेश्वर विश्वरूप ॥ १६ ॥

Aneka-bāhūdara-vakra-netraṁ
paśyāmi tvāṁ sarvato-'nanta-rūpam,
nāntaṁ na madhyaṁ na punas-tavādiṁ
paśyāmi viśveśvara viśvarūpa.

अनेक-बाहु-उदर-वक्त्र-नेत्रम् *aneka-bāhu-udara-vakra-netram* = with manifold arms, stomachs, mouths and eyes; पश्यामि *paśyāmi* = (I) see; त्वाम् *tvām* = thee; सर्वतः *sarvataḥ* = on every side; अनन्त-रूपम् *ananta-rūpam* = of boundless form; न *na* = not; अन्तम् *antam* = end; न *na* = not; मध्यम् *madhyam* = middle; न *na* = not; पुनः *punaḥ* = again; तव *tava* = thy; आदिम् *ādim* = origin; पश्यामि *paśyāmi* = (I) see; विश्वेश्वर *viśveśvara* = O Lord of the Universe; विश्वरूप *viśvarūpa* = O cosmic form.

16. *I see Thee of boundless form on every side, with manifold arms, stomachs, mouths and eyes; neither Thy end, nor the middle, nor also the beginning do I see; O! Lord of the Universe, O! Cosmic-Form.*

A limited human intellect is not the instrument with which one can perceive in one sweep the Infinite majesty of the Universal-Form. It must necessarily stand staggered at the vastness of the concept and the significances of Its sheer dimensions. That the Lord is the *one* dynamic Truth behind every organ of activity and in every existent thing is indicated here when *Arjuna* says "*I see Thee of boundless form on every side, with manifold arms, stomachs, mouths and eyes.*" This is not to be construed as a caricature of Truth. This warning is necessary for all hasty artists, who, inspired by the theme, generally rush to this field of thought, to represent this Cosmic Form with their brushes and colours. And they all but fail miserably!

The Universal Oneness is not an object of perception; it is only a fact to be realised or apprehended. This is endorsed by the very words of *Arjuna* that immediately follow in the stanza, "*neither Thy end, nor the middle, nor also the beginning do I see.*" The description of the Truth—from which all names and forms arise, in which they exist, and into which they all merge back at the end of their temporary play—cannot be better done in any other way and those who, with sympathetic understanding, get at the real import of these stanzas can appreciate their rich beauties and luxurious warmth.

The above stanzas express the oneness that threads through the mortal beings and finite things of the world, making a single garland of them all!

It may be doubted whether the deified denizens of the divine hierarchy are also represented upon this wonder form. This is answered in the following:

किरीटिनं गदिनं चक्रिणं च
तेजोराशिं सर्वतो दीप्तिमन्तम् ।
पश्यामि त्वां दुर्निरीक्ष्यं समन्तात्
दीप्तानलार्कद्युतिमप्रमेयम् ॥ १७ ॥

Kirīṭinaṁ gadinaṁ cakriṇaṁ ca
tejorāśiṁ sarvato dīpti-mantam,
paśyāmi tvāṁ dur-nirīkṣyaṁ samantāt
dīptāna-lārka-dhyutima-prameyam.

किरीटिनम् *kirīṭinam* = one with diadem (crown); गदिनम् *gadinam* = with club; चक्रिणम् *cakriṇam* = with discus; च *ca* = and; तेजो राशिम् *tejo rāśim* = a mass of radiance; सर्वत: *sarvataḥ* = everywhere; दीप्तिमन्तम् *dīptimantam* = shining; पश्यामि *paśyāmi* = (I) see; त्वाम् *tvām* = thee; दुर्निरीक्ष्यम् *dur-nirīkṣyam* = very hard to looked at; समन्तात् *samantāt* = all round; दीप्त-अनल-अर्क द्युतिम् *dīpta-anala-arka-dhyutim* = blazing like burning fire and sun; अप्रमेयम् *aprameyam* = incomprehensible.

17. *I see Thee with Crown, Club, and Discus; a mass of radiance shining everywhere, very hard to look*

at, all round blazing like burning fire and Sun, and incomprehensible.

Continuing his description of the Cosmic-Form, the *Pāṇḍava* Prince gives more and more details of what he comprehends in that incomprehensible Divine extravaganza. He sees therein the Crown, the Club, and the Discus. These are the insignia which Lord *Viṣṇu* is said to carry, in all mythological descriptions.

Hindū gods are represented as having certain divine symbols, and they all have their own respective special significances—of Kingship and Lordliness over the world of finite things and happenings. He alone is the Lord who is a Master-of-circumstances and a Ruler-of-impulses. A slave to life and its enchantments is a weakling, on whose head a crown rests only temporarily like the gilted-cardboard-crown of an actor playing on a stage. No authority or effectiveness in life is possible unless the man-in-power has self-control and self-mastery. No man can live a happy and mighty life unless he has conquered his passions and crowned himself with kingship over himself. He is *Viṣṇu* and He alone deserves the crown!

The four-armed *Viṣṇu* carries in his hands the Conch, the Discus, the Club, and the Lotus. This is extremely symbolical. In India the Lotus represents "peace and joy, auspiciousness and happiness." The Conch blows and calls man to duty; and if there be a generation of men who listen not to the Higher-call in themselves, restlessness, war, pestilence, famine, storms, and chaotic social and communal disturbances visit them—the Club descends to hammer the generation to shape and discipline. Even after this punishment, if there be a generation so totally dissipated that it cannot improve, then comes the Discus—the sharp-toothed wheel, ever revolving, the Whirling of Time (*Kāla-cakra*) to annihilate the irredeemable generation.

When we find these in *Arjuna*'s description as part of the Universal Form, it becomes evident that the same Truth is the Substratum, not only of the lowest of low worms, but even of the Divine Trinity. The Eternal Truth is one and the same, everywhere, at all times; only Its manifestations are varied, and the degree of Divinity sparkling from each differs according to the grossness or subtlety of the equipment through which the same Infinite Reality expresses Itself.

As a mass of radiance shining everywhere, very hard to look at, all round blazing like burning fire and sun:—One of the most expressive lines in this description, this brings home to us the glory of Pure Awareness. This is not 'light' in the physical sense of the term; but all the same we have to use the word, borrowed from ordinary language, though it is applied here with a special significance. Consciousness is the 'Light' in which we so clearly 'see' our own thoughts and emotions. It is the same light which, beaming out through the eyes, throws 'light' upon the world and illumines for us the *forms and shapes*. The same Consciousness, beaming out through the ears, with its special 'light,' illumines *sound*, and so on. Naturally, therefore, the Universal-Form of *Kṛṣṇa*, representing in Himself the Infinite Awareness, had to be described, in the faltering language of *Arjuna*, as a mass of resplendent light, blinding all faculties of perception, feeling and understanding.

Incomprehensible (*Aprameya*)—So far, though *Arjuna* described, as best as he could, the Form, and the feelings It had engendered in him, there is a streak of despair running in these stanzas. *Arjuna* feels that he has not captured the theme fully in the web of his language. Language expresses that which is perceived, or felt, or understood. Here is a form which *Arjuna* experiences. He beholds. He feels. And he comprehends it in himself. Yet, strangely enough, here is an experience that volatilizes and eludes all attempts at being bottled in language! He seems to be not satisfied by the objective description which he gave in the language of his eyes, ears, etc., and he feels equally unhappy with the language of his emotion, as felt by his mind.

True to himself, the wonder-struck mortal is trying to sing the glory of what he lives, in the language of his intellect. But even here he can only cry in despair, "*Oh Lord thou art ever incomprehensible.*" Though the Universal Form is painted here by the author, in the language of an "objective experience," he makes us understand that the Truth is the *subject* and not an *object* of even the intellect. The Self is *the knower, the feeler, the perceiver*; It is not the perceived, the felt, or the known.

From this vision of thy power of Yoga, *I infer:*

त्वमक्षरं परमं वेदितव्यं
त्वमस्य विश्वस्य परं निधानम् ।
त्वमव्ययः शाश्वतधर्मगोप्ता
सनातनस्त्वं पुरुषो मतो मे ॥ १८ ॥

Tvam-akṣaraṁ paramaṁ veditavyaṁ
tvam-asya viśvasya paraṁ nidhānam,
tvama-vyayaḥ śāśvata-dharma-goptā
sanātanas-tvaṁ puruṣo mato me.

त्वम् *tvam* = you; अक्षरम् *akṣaram* = imperishable; परमम् *paramam* = the supreme being; वेदितव्यम् *veditavyam* = worthy to be known; त्वम् *tvam* = you; अस्य *asya* = (of) this; विश्वस्य *viśvasya* = of universe; परम् *param* = the great; निधानम् *nidhānam* = treasure-house; त्वम् *tvam* = you; अव्ययः *avyayaḥ* = imperishable; शाश्वत-धर्म-गोप्ता *śāśvata-dharma-goptā* = protector of the Eternal *Dharma*; सनातनः *sanātanaḥ* = ancient; त्वम् *tvam* = you; पुरुषः *puruṣaḥ* = *Puruṣa*; मतः *mataḥ* = opinion; मे *me* = by me, my.

18. *You are the Imperishable, the Supreme Being worthy to be known. You are the great treasure-house of this Universe. You are the imperishable Protector of the Eternal* Dharma. *In my opinion, You are the Ancient* Puruṣa.

From every experience, all intelligent men try to gather their own conclusions, which alone, in fact, constitute true knowledge. *Arjuna* had a great experience, too subtle for words to express, or for his intellect to comprehend, in all its entirety. But from what he saw, he tries to draw certain conclusions. Crystallised into his understanding, the conclusions are that the Power behind this Cosmic Form is that which is the Imperishable Supreme Truth.

When we see all the waves playing on the surface of the ocean, manifesting and disappearing after a temporary existence into the very waters from which they rose, we generally conclude that the ocean is the source of all waves. It becomes at once the rest-house for the waves, or the treasure-house for all the disturbances. Similarly, *Arjuna* comes to the intelligent conclusion that *Kṛṣṇa*, as the Cosmic-Form, is the very Substratum from which the pluralistic world of phenomena arises, exists in, and merges into. The Universe (*Viśva*) mentioned here, is not merely the astronomers' universe of physical things, but, in *Vedānta*, *Viśva* is the sum-total experience of everyone, gained through the individual instruments of perception, feeling and understanding. The Lord is the foundation (*Nidhānam*) for the entire universe of disturbances, experienced by us at our physical, mental and intellectual levels.

Things that change can continue to do so only on a changeless substratum. The world-of-change plays ever to the tune of Time and Space. But, in order that we may feel a continuity of the happenings and thereby gain a comprehensive experience of the total, there must be one constant and changeless "Knowing-principle" that registers the happenings, without itself in the least being involved in the change. That truth is the Self, and the Self alone is that which could take upon itself the stupendous Universal-Form (*Viśvarūpa*). Keeping these ideas in mind, *Arjuna* declares that He who has transformed Himself into this Wonder-Form is the One Changeless Truth, that permeates the entire realm of changes and modifications.

You are the Imperishable Protector (deathless Guardian) of the Eternal Dharma (*Śāśvata-dharma-goptā*):—Even though the theme is so mighty and the delineation so unique, the giant intellect of *Vyāsa* finds it almost a pleasant afternoon-game, wherein his artistic thirst to add beauty never gets dampened even for once. He is at ease. Here is an instance of the incomparable beauty in the artistic turn of his words: so expressive, so economical and so significant. The term "Eternal-*Dharma-Guardian*" is so happily blended, that it can be "*Guardian of the* Eternal *Dharma*" or " *the Eternal Guardian of Dharma*" or "*Eternal Guardian of the Eternal Dharma.*" The term "*Dharma*" was already explained earlier in our discourse. Since the Divine Self is the true nature of man and the Self is Eternal and All-pervading, the *Hindū Dharma* is rightly called "*the Eternal Dharma*" (*Sanātana Dharma*).

In India, to the *Hindū-s*, the protector of his *Dharma* is not a mortal king, or a priest class. The Supreme alone is its guardian, for the *Hindū-s* are not followers of any accidental prophet, who had a fleeting historical reality and a limited mission of serving his immediate generation with the best he had. To the *Hindū*, the Eternal Truth is his goal, his Master and his way. We demand no mortal power with its poison-gas and atom-bomb to protect our *Dharma*. Nor do we need any organised army of men who have been perverted to believe that "Our God is the only Lord" and "our Prophet alone is the only Saviour" and "our seats get reserved in the Heavens if we convert, by means both fair and foul, a few of the infidels!"

That You are the ancient Puruṣa, is my opinion:—In *Vedānta*, the very physical structure is considered as a Capital-city with nine gates, each controlled and guarded by its presiding deity. That which dwells in the city, here meaning the body, is called '*Puruṣa*' in *Saṁskṛta*. In the context of the stanza, it only means that the solution for the riddle of life, which is the source, or substratum of the whole universe, is to be sought, not among the world-of-objects but within the very layers of personalities in us, until we discover it as the

Puruṣa, the Eternal. The Conscious Principle, which is the Spark-of-life in everyone, is here indicated to be the very Eternal Truth which alone can take up the Form-Universal, as it stands now in front of *Arjuna*'s bewildered gaze.

Moreover:

अनादिमध्यान्तमनन्तवीर्यम्
अनन्तबाहुं शशिसूर्यनेत्रम् ।
पश्यामि त्वां दीप्तहुताशवक्त्रं
स्वतेजसा विश्वमिदं तपन्तम् ॥ १९ ॥

Anādi-madhyānta-mananta-vīryam
ananta-bāhuṁ śaśi-sūrya-netram,
paśyāmi tvāṁ dīpta-hutāśa-vaktraṁ
sva-tejasā viśva-midaṁ tapantam.

अनादि मध्य अन्तम् *anādi madhya antam* = without beginning, middle or end; अनन्त-वीर्यम् *ananta-vīryam* = infinite in power; अनन्त-बाहुम् *ananta-bāhum* = of infinite (endless) arms; शशि-सूर्य-नेत्रम् *śaśi-sūrya-netram* = the sun and the moon (your) eyes; पश्यामि *paśyāmi* = (I) see; त्वाम् *tvām* = you; दीप्त हुताश वक्त्रम् *dīpta hutāśa vaktram* = the burning fire of (your) mouth; स्वतेजसा *sva-tejasā* = with (your) own radiance; विश्वम् *viśvam* = the universe; इदम् *idam* = this; तपन्तम् *tapantam* = heating.

19. *I see You without beginning, middle, or end, infinite in power, of infinite (endless) arms, the sun and moon being (Your) eyes, the burning fire (Your) mouth, heating the whole universe with (Your) own radiance.*

Continuing the description of the Infinite as comprehended by the subtle perception of *Arjuna* and interpreted by his intellect in terms of the Universe of things and names, it is explained, "*I see thee without beginning, middle and end, infinite in power, of infinite arms.*" This pen-picture, drawn by *Vyāsa* with his eloquent poetry, gives a false impression that the theme is an object, and many are the artists who have tried to capture this form on the canvas. The folly is clear to every intelligent student of *Vedānta*. That which is Infinite, without beginning or end, cannot be brought within the area of a limited canvas-piece. But, at the same time, the phrase "*of infinite arms*" tickles the painter to express it through his own art. In fact, the Universal-Form, standing out so clearly in relief work in this transcendental apprehension of the author, can be comprehended only by students of deep understanding and developed intuition.

Here, by the term "*of infinite arms*" it only means that the Supreme Self, as the dynamic life, is the one essential strength behind every hand that acts and achieves.

The Sun and the Moon being (Your) eyes:—Some commentators attribute that the Lord's sun-eye is for chastisement and His moon-eye is for blessing the generation. This is a meaning that has been pressed out by over-straining the text and this is unfair to the *Gītā*. The Sun and the Moon together represent the source of the entire light energy; the Sun representing the source of all light and the moon representing all the reflected and otherwise conditioned light. In describing that the eyes of the Universal Form are constituted of the Sun and the Moon, it only implies the oneness of the individual and the cosmic.

The "principle of light" is the very "principle" in the eye. If the eyes were not there, light itself would have no meaning. At the same time, if the "principle of light" were not blessing the objects of form, the instruments of cognition—the eyes—could not have functioned at all. We have here the description of the totality. The "principle of vision" i.e., all the eyes in the whole universe, is described as the pair-of-eyes, in the Universal-Form of the Lord. Therefore, in the technical language of *Vedānta*, it has been aptly described here that "*the sun and the moon being Your eyes.*"

Burning fire Your mouth:—Here fire has been considered as the principle behind speech and the principle governing taste. Warm food tastes better; frozen-food has no taste. The presiding deity of speech can *fire* the generation. *Heated* discussions always take place; cold discussion is a painful monotony. Speeches that freeze the audience are only lullabies. And the mouth being the seat for both the instruments of speech and taste, the mouth of the *Viśvarūpa* is explained here as "Fire."

Heating the whole universe with (Your) own radiance:—The Self cannot but be luminous, because Consciousness illumines all experiences, at all times, in all living organisms. This light of Consciousness not only illumines, but also imparts the warmth of life to the entire Universe. From the very statement it is evident that the ancient *Hindū* had turned his gaze inward only when he had exhausted his observations and study of the world outside. It seems that he knew well that at a certain degree of temperature alone life could continue on this globe; below the required minimum and above the maximum temperature, life would be extinct.

The light that is emanating from Truth is Its own light, and not something which It has derived from any other source. It is by "*Your own Radiance*" (*Sva-Tejasā*) that the life is sustained in the world of names and forms.

Objective descriptions have always in them the danger of others misunderstanding that the Truth so described is limited both by time and space.

Vyāsa is ever conscious of this, and he is never tired of repeating, again and again, within each stanza and also in between the stanzas, direct statements and precise indications, that what is described here is the Infinite, All-pervading Truth itself. The following is an example:

द्यावापृथिव्योरिदमन्तरं हि
व्याप्तं त्वयैकेन दिशश्च सर्वाः ।
दृष्ट्वाद्भुतं रूपमुग्रं तवेदं
लोकत्रयं प्रव्यथितं महात्मन् ॥ २० ॥

Dyāvā-pṛthivyo-rida-mantaraṁ hi
vyāptaṁ tvayai-kena diśaś-ca sarvāḥ,
dṛṭvād-bhutaṁ rūpa-mugraṁ tavedaṁ
loka-trayaṁ pra-vyathitaṁ mahātman.

द्यावा-पृथिव्यः dyāvā-pṛthivyaḥ = of heaven and earth; इदम् *idam* = this; अन्तरम् *antaram* = inter-space; हि *hi* = indeed; व्याप्तम् *vyāptam* = are filled; त्वया *tvayā* = by you; एकेन *ekena* = alone; दिशः *diśaḥ* = quarters; च *ca* = and; सर्वाः *sarvāḥ* = all; दृष्ट्वा *dṛṭvā* = having seen; अद्भुतम् *adbhutam* = wonderful; रूपम् *rūpam* = form; उग्रम् *ugram* = terrible; तव *tava* = your; इदम् *idam* = this; लोक-त्रयम् *loka-trayam* = the three worlds; प्रव्यथितम् *pravyathitam* = are trembling with fear; महात्मन् *mahātman* = O! *Mahātman,* great souled being.

20. *This space between the earth and the heavens and all the quarters is filled by You alone; having seen this, Your wonderful and terrible form, the three worlds are trembling with fear, O great-souled Being.*

Truth, as apprehended by *Arjuna*, pervades the entire world-of-objects and even the concepts of time and space are not independent of this Truth. The theme that has been described here, we should not forget, is the Infinite, the Eternal. Naturally, it is said here, "*by You alone, the space between heaven and earth and all the quarters of the sky, is pervaded.*"

The concept of universal oneness cannot be easily grasped. The more one realises it, the more one gets staggered at the immensity of it all. A limited intellect cannot but shudder at the manifestation of such a vast and majestic Truth.

Seeing the marvellous and the awful form, *Arjuna* says, "*the worlds are trembling.*" It is psychologically true that each man sees the world as he himself is. We look at the world through the windows of our mind; as our mind is, so is the world to us. *Arjuna* felt staggered and trembling in himself when he looked at the world in that mental condition, and he could not but see that the whole world was equally wonder-struck and trembling as he himself was. Even while he is pre-occupied with the great theme in hand, *Vyāsa* does not forget the fundamental behaviour in man. These fine touches add a glow of realism to this mystic picture of incomparable beauty and immeasurable depth.

Arjuna *had doubt regarding the possibilities of success in the war.* In order to remove this, Lord* Kṛṣṇa *now gives* Arjuna *a peep into the future that is in store for the world:*

अमी हि त्वां सुरसंघा विशन्ति
केचिद्भीताः प्राञ्जलयो गृणन्ति ।
स्वस्तीत्युक्त्वा महर्षिसिद्धसंघाः
स्तुवन्ति त्वां स्तुतिभिः पुष्कलाभिः ॥ २१ ॥

Amī hi tvāṁ surasaṁghā viśanti
kecid-bhītāḥ prāñjalayo gṛṇanti,
svastī-tyuktvā maharṣi-siddha-saṁghāḥ
stuvanti tvāṁ stutibhiḥ puṣkalābhiḥ.

अमी *amī* = these; हि *hi* = verily; त्वाम् *tvām* = (into) you; सुरसंघाः *sura-saṁghāḥ* = hosts of *Devā-s*; विशन्ति *viśanti* = enter; केचित् *kecit* = some; भीताः *bhītāḥ* = in fear; प्राञ्जलयः *prāñjalayaḥ* = with joined palms; गृणन्ति *gṛṇanti* = extol; स्वस्ति *svasti* = may it be well; इति *iti* = thus; उक्त्वा *uktvā* = having said; महर्षि-सिद्ध-संघाः *maharṣi-siddha-saṁghāḥ* = bands of great *Ṛṣī-s* and *Siddhā-s*; स्तुवन्ति

* "*Yadvā jayema yadi-vā no jayeyuḥ*"—*Gītā* II-6.

stuvanti = praise; त्वाम् *tvām* = you; स्तुतिभिः *stutibhiḥ* = with hymns; पुष्कलाभिः *puṣkalābhiḥ* = sublime.

21. Verily, into You enter these hosts of Devā-s; *some extol You in fear with joined palms; "May it be well" thus saying, bands of great* Ṛṣī-s *and* Siddhā-s *praise You with hymns sublime.*

The running commentary given out so long by *Arjuna* was the description of a stagnant Cosmic-Form, at once "marvellous and awful." Here we find *Arjuna* describing the movements and actions that he observes in that Cosmic-Form of the Lord. "*These hosts of deities*" enter into and disappear in the Universal-Form. *Śaṅkara*, commenting upon the expression "*Hosts of deities*," interprets it to mean the *Duryodhana*-fold. Though this interpretation is not inconsistent with what is yet to follow, it is true that this meaning is not the natural interpretation of the terms used in the text.

If some, who are thus irredeemably drawn towards the Lord's Form, disappear therein, others who are waiting and watching the process are necessarily getting panicky with fear. When man is threatened with a sure mishap, and when he knows of no remedy or defence against it, he, in his despair, always turns to prayer. This psychological truth is beautifully brought out here, when it explains how "*some in fear extol Thee with joined palms.*"

And this is not all. Bands of great *Ṛṣī-s* and perfected-men (*Siddhā-s*)[1] who are not at all perturbed by the Vision of the Totality, because of their super-human tranquillity and inward peace arising from their own "wisdom," merely sing "sublime"[2] hymns of glory to the mighty appearance of the total phenomenal world of multiplicity. They do so wishing "*may it be well*" to all, always. They realise in

1. It is believed that there are about, 18,000 such perfect Masters, who are godly in their wisdom, and are ever-serving the cause of the Life Divine and guiding subtly each seeker towards his consummate goal.
2. *Śaṅkara* interprets '*Puṣkalābhiḥ*' as meaning complete. Both meanings are possible.

their "wisdom" that the face of the Cosmos assumes such a terrible ferocity only when it has launched a wholesale reconstruction scheme. The Men of Wisdom also know that nothing is lost in such a programme of "construction through destruction." Therefore, they hail this process and wish the world a brilliant golden era, which is sure to follow immediately after such a total upheaval.

In this stanza, the entire world of phenomena has been beautifully brought under three heads: the "Sub-normal," the "Normal," and the "Super-normal." The "Sub-normal" unconsciously die away. They are the victims of the process of death and they are so miserably unaware of the very process, that they do not at all revolt against it. The "Normal" dread when they intelligently observe and become aware of the process of decay and death. They become apprehensive of their own fate; and failing to realise that nothing is lost by death, they, in their ignorance, shudder at the inescapable lot of all living names and forms.

There is yet another set constituted of "Super-normal" men, who have sufficient apprehension of the Totality and Its behaviour, and who are not at all perturbed even if what is happening in the Universe everyday, were to visit them also one day. When bubbles are broken, there is no occasion to regret for those who know what they are and how they are born. Similarly, when these *Siddhā-s* see the upheaval that precedes a dying culture's reorientation, they recognise therein the mighty Power of Truth and wish only good luck and peace to the world so reconstructed by the very hands of the Lord.

In whichever light we may observe this work, we must come to realise how great a psychologist *Vyāsa* himself must have been and also how beautifully the knowledge of the mental behaviour has been harnessed for quickening the evolution of man to reach the fulfilment of all his struggles.

How then did the gods of the heavens react to this spectacular vision of the cosmic-man in action?

रुद्रादित्या वसवो ये च साध्या
विश्वेऽश्विनौ मरुतश्चोष्मपाश्च ।
गन्धर्वयक्षासुर सिद्धसंघा
वीक्षन्ते त्वां विस्मिताश्चैव सर्वे ॥ २२ ॥

Rudrā-dityā vasavo ye ca sādhyā
viśve-'śvinau marutaś-coṣmapāś-ca,
gandharva-yakṣāsura-siddha-saṁghā
vīkṣante tvāṁ vismitāś-caiva sarve.

रुद्र–आदित्याः *rudra-ādityāḥ* = *Rudrā-s* and *Ādityā-s;* वसवः *vasavaḥ* = *Vasū-s;* ये *ye* = these; च *ca* = and; साध्याः *sādhyāḥ* = *Sādhyā-s;* विश्वे *viśve* = *Viśvedevā-s;* अश्विनौ *aśvinau* = the (two) *Aśvin-s;* मरुतः *marutaḥ* = *Maruta-s;* च *ca* = and; ऊष्मपाः *uṣmapāḥ* = *pitṛ-s;* च *ca* = and; गन्धर्व यक्ष असुर सिद्ध संघाः *gandharva yakṣa asura siddha saṁghāḥ* = hosts of *Gandarvā-s, Yakṣā-s, Asurā-s* and *Siddhā-s;* वीक्षन्ते *vīkṣante* = are looking at; त्वाम् *tvām* = you; विस्मिताः *vismitāḥ* = astonished; च *ca* = and; एव *eva* = even; सर्वे *sarve* = all.

22. *The* Rudrā-s, Ādityā-s, Vasū-s, Sādhyā-s, Viśvedevā-s, Aśvin-s, Maruta-s, Uṣmapā-s *and hosts of* Gandharvā-s, Yakṣā-s, Asurā-s *and* Siddhā-s—*they are all looking at You, all quite astonished.*

Continuing the description, *Arjuna* says that among the hosts of beings who gaze on at the Mysterious Form, there are *Deities* who are all the Lords of the phenomena, worshipped and revered by the generations of the *Vedik* period. Even they, looking at the Universal Form, stand struck with wonder and astonishment.

The terms used here have all been described during our discourses on the previous chapters. The Spirits of Destruction (*Rudrā-s*), the Sun (*Ādityā-s*), the Lord of the

Seasons (*Vasū-s*), the Spirits of the Sky (*Sādhyā-s*),[1] the Lesser Lords (*Viśve-devā-s*),[2] the Horsemen Twins (*Aśvin-s*), the Storm-Lords (*Marutā-s*), the Heat-drinkers (*Uṣmapā-s*),[3] the hosts of Heavenly Musicians (*Gandharvā-s*), *Yakṣā-s*, *Asurā-s* and *Siddhā-s*—these constitute the crowd that gaze at the terrible form of the Lord, "*all quite astonished.*"

This stanza may not be quite appealing to us who are today strangers to the conceptions which these terms represent. But *Arjuna* was a student of the *Vedā-s*, and was the child of the age; he was naturally well-versed in these *Vedik* thoughts and therefore the vocabulary of *Arjuna* could not have been otherwise. We have only to watch for, and understand, the general effect produced upon the *Pāṇḍava* warrior by the Vision of the Totality and the different reactions created in different types of minds. Each, according to its own intrinsic capacity, comprehended and appreciated the Vision of the entire Universe, so crystallised into the definite shapeless shape.

Giving more and more sure strokes, Arjuna *is bringing out his experiences to a precise conception upon the canvas of his listener's mind:*

रूपं महत्ते बहुवक्त्रनेत्रं
महाबाहो बहुबाहूरुपादम् ।
बहूदरं बहुदंष्ट्राकरालं
दृष्ट्वा लोकाः प्रव्यथितास्तथाहम् ॥ २३ ॥

---

1. Refer *Ṛg Veda* X-90-15. They are personifications of sacrificial rites and prayers: they are, as it were, the 'divine middle men' who convey the devotees' prayers to that Lord to whom they were raised and ultimately bring about the fruition of the desires entertained by the devotees.
2. This is a collective name for a set of inferior deities mentioned in the *Ṛg Veda*. In the *Purāṇā-s*, we find mention of these deities, where it is considered that they are altogether ten in number. They include abstract qualities like *Satya, Dhṛti*, etc.
3. This is a term used to indicate the dead ancestors—*Pitṛ-s*—who are supposed to be 'heat-drinkers' in as much as it is believed that they come during functions dedicated to them and enjoy the offerings made to them only so long it is hot. The idea, perhaps, must be that they take only the fragrance that rolls up the steaming food offered.

Rūpaṁ mahatte bahu-vaktra-netraṁ
mahā-bāho bahu-bāhū-rupādam,
bahū-daraṁ bahu-daṁṣṭrā-karālaṁ
dṛṣtvā lokāḥ pravya-thitās-tathāham.

रूपम् *rūpam* = form; महत् *mahat* = immeasurable; ते *te* = your; बहु-वक्त्र नेत्रम् *bahu vaktra netram* = with many mouths and eyes; महा बाहो *mahā bāho* = O mighty-armed; बहु बाहुरु पादम् *bahu bāhuru pādam* = with many arms, thighs and feet; बहु उदरम् *bahu udaram* = with many stomachs; बहु दंष्ट्रा करालम् *bahu daṁṣṭrā karālam* = fearsome with many tusks; दृष्ट्वा *dṛṣtvā* = having seen; लोकाः *lokāḥ* = the worlds; प्रव्यथिताः *pravyathitāḥ* = are terrified; तथा *tathā* = also; अहम् *aham* = I.

23. *Having seen Your immeasurable form, with many mouths and eyes, O Mighty-armed, with many arms, thighs, and feet, with many stomachs and fearsome with many tusks—the worlds are terrified and so am I too.*

नभःस्पृशं दीप्तमनेकवर्णं
व्यात्ताननं दीप्तविशालनेत्रम् ।
दृष्ट्वा हि त्वां प्रव्यथितान्तरात्मा
धृतिं न विन्दामि शमं च विष्णो ॥ २४ ॥

Nabhaḥ-spṛśaṁ dīptam-aneka-varṇaṁ
vyāttā-nanaṁ dīpta-viśāla-netram,
dṛṣṭvā hi tvāṁ pra-vyathit-āntarātmā
dhṛtiṁ na vindāmi śamaṁ ca viṣṇo.

नभः स्पृशम् *nabhaḥ spṛśam* = touching the sky; दीप्तम् *dīptam* = flaming, shining; अनेक वर्णम् *aneka varṇam* = in many colours; व्यात्ताननम् *vyāttānanam* = with mouths wide open; दीप्त विशाल नेत्रम् *dīpta viśāla netram* = with large fiery eyes; दृष्ट्वा *dṛṣtvā* = having seen; हि *hi* = verily; त्वाम् *tvām* = you; प्रव्यथित-अन्तरात्मा *pravyathita-*

antarātmā = terrified at heart; धृतिम् *dhṛtim* = courage; न *na* = not; विन्दामि *vindāmi* = (I) find; शमम् *śamam* = peace; च *ca* = and; विष्णो *visṇo* = O *Viṣṇu.*

24. *On seeing You, with Your Form touching the sky, flaming in many colours, with mouths wide open, with large fiery eyes, I am terrified at heart, and I find neither courage, nor peace,* O Viṣṇu!

The uncommon vision, "marvellous and awful," experienced by *Arjuna,* was not a localised form on a six-footed Lord *Kṛṣṇa.* It was, in fact, a manifestation, wide and varied, extending almost to the frontiers of the All-pervading. And yet, the *Pāṇḍava* Prince realised it all in his inward vision as a limited form, having a definite shape. In the intellectual understanding of all shapeless qualities (like freedom, love, nationality, etc.), one gives them each a substantiality, a form, well-defined and precisely outlined for one's own intellect, although never for one's own sense-organs. Similarly, *Arjuna* too feels that, the experience of the Universal-Form, though All-pervading, has for him a definite shape. But when he tries to define the Form-Universal, so well realised by him, his very expressions belie his own feelings and defeat his own purpose.

Arjuna finds that the entire world is terrified by the Great Grand Form representing in itself "*many mouths and eyes, many arms thighs and feet, with many stomachs, and fearsome with many tusks.*" He also adds, "*so am I.*" Psychologically, when an individual is in a crowd of excited people or in the company of good men of peaceful contemplation, he vicariously gathers unto himself the mental qualities of the crowd in which he finds himself. "*The world is terrified,*" and, *Arjuna* confesses, "*so am I too.*"

At the same time, the *Pāṇḍava* Prince feels it insulting and cowardly for his royal heart to feel any fear. Therefore, justifying his own fear, he describes the Terrible-Form to be in fact formless, and says that it absorbs into itself everything. The Universal-Form touches the very skies above. It glows with a variety of colours. Its fiery-eyes glow. Its open mouths consume everything. Altogether, the vision is capable of unnerving even the gods. Seeing that 'Vision' *Arjuna* confesses, "*I am terrified at heart, and I find neither courage, nor peace.*" It is very significant that it is in this condition of benumbing fear that the great hero addresses the cosmic-vision, "*O! Viṣṇu.*"*

As I said in the beginning, the conception-form so clearly defined in the intuitive understanding of *Arjuna*, is in fact the Infinite described in terms of Its own endless manifestations as the names and forms in the Universe. We, the students of the *Gītā*, should never forget these subtle under-currents of thought that *Vyāsa* has so secretly kept for the profit of all diligent and sincere seekers of Truth.

Elaborating his own self-explanations on why heroic hearts should tremble in fear, the Paṇḍava *Prince continues:*

दंष्ट्राकरालानि च ते मुखानि
दृष्ट्वैव कालानलसन्निभानि ।
दिशो न जाने न लभे च शर्म
प्रसीद देवेश जगन्निवास ॥ २५ ॥

Daṁṣṭrā-karālāni ca te mukhāni
dṛṣṭ-vaiva kālānala-sannibhāni,
diśo na jāne na labhe ca śarma
prasīda deveśa jagan-nivāsa.

---

* The term *Viṣṇu* appears in the *Vedik* literature where it is used in its etymological meaning as "one having long strides." The measure between the two feet, when one walks, is called the stride (or reach). The stride of a child is short when compared with the stride of a man. The All-pervading Infinite, if it were to take its longest stride, should be from the "beginningless" to the "endless." Thus, the term *Viṣṇu* has the implication of "the All-Pervading."

दंष्ट्रा-करालानि *daṁṣṭrā-karālāni* = fearful with tusks; च *ca* = and; ते *te* = your; मुखानि *mukhāni* = mouths; दृष्ट्वा *dṛṣṭvā* = having seen; एव *eva* = even; काल-अनल-सन्निभानि *kāla-anala-sannibhāni* = blazing like *Pralaya*-fires; दिशः *diśaḥ* = the four quarters; न *na* = not; जाने *jāne* = know; न *na* = not; लभे *labhe* = do (I) find; च *ca* = and; शर्म *śarma* = peace; प्रसीद *prasīda* = be gracious; देवेश *deveśa* = O Lord of the *Devā-s;* जगत्-निवास *jagat-nivāsa* = O abode of the Universe.

25. *Having seen Your mouths fearsome with tusks (blazing) like* Pralaya *fires, I know not the four quarters, nor do I find peace; be gracious, O Lord of the* Devā-s, *O Abode of the Universe.*

"Seeing the universal-mouth terrible with tusks, threatening as the fires-of-deluge," confesses *Arjuna*, *"I have lost my sense of direction and I feel no peace."* This is the picture of Time—Time, the leveller of everything, the consumer of all forms. When the intellect comes to comprehend such a vast field, and that too all of a sudden, the very magnitude of it smothers all powers of discrimination and benumbs the individual for a moment. This chaotic condition of confusion is expressed here, *"I know not the four quarters."* And this is not all, *"nor do I find peace"* either.

In such a condition of extreme wonderment, the astounded mortal comes to realise that his physical might, his mental capacities and his intellectual subtleties are all, both individually and in their aggregate, unimportant vehicles indeed. The little ego drops down its veil of vanity and its armour of false strength, and stands naked meekly surrendering itself to the influence of the Cosmic-Power. Prayer is the only resort of the individual, who has thus fully realised the emptiness of his own hollow vanities, in the presence of the Mighty-Total and the Supreme-Divine.

In concluding the stanza with the humble prayer, *"be gracious, O Lord, thou art the Abode of the Universe,"* *Vyāsa* has rightly indicated that true prayers can never rise up from a heart that is swollen with pride and entertains an exaggerated sense of self-importance. Only when man understands his own individual insignificance, in the context of the total Universe, then true prayer can rise up from him almost involuntarily.

This particular section (Starting from XI-21) is mainly for reassuring Arjuna *of the success that is yet to come in the future for himself and his army. Therefore, the Lord directly shows the forces enter the inescapable "mouth of time" and disappear:*

अमी च त्वां धृतराष्ट्रस्य पुत्राः
सर्वे सहैवावनिपालसंघैः ।
भीष्मो द्रोणः सूतपुत्रस्तथासौ
सहास्मदीयैरपि योधमुख्यैः ॥ २६ ॥

Amī ca tvāṁ dṛtarāṣṭrasya putrāḥ
sarve sahaivā-vanipāla-saṁghaiḥ,
bhīṣmo droṇaḥ sūta-putras-tathāsau
sahā-smadī-yairapi yodha-mukhaiḥ.

अमी *amī* = these; च *ca* = and; त्वाम् *tvām* = you; धृतराष्ट्रस्य *dṛtarāṣṭrasya* = of *Dṛtarāṣṭra*; पुत्राः *putrāḥ* = sons; सर्वे *sarve* = all; सह *saha* = with; एव *eva* = even; अवनिपाल-संङ्घैः *avani-pāla-saṁghaiḥ* = hosts of kings of the earth; भीष्मः *bhīṣmaḥ* = *Bhīṣma*; द्रोणः *droṇaḥ* = *Droṇa*; सूतपुत्रः *sūta-putraḥ* = son of the charioteer, *Karṇa*; तथा *tathā* = also; असौ *asau* = this; सह *saha* = with; अस्मदीयैः *asmadīyaiḥ* = with (those) of ours; अपि *api* = also; योध-मुख्यैः *yodha-mukhaiḥ* = (with) warrior chiefs.

26. *All the sons of* Dhṛtarāṣṭra *with hosts of kings of the earth,* Bhīṣma, Droṇa *and the son of a charioteer,* Karṇa, *with the warrior chieftains of ours;*

वक्त्राणि ते त्वरमाणा विशन्ति
दंष्ट्राकरालानि भयानकानि ।
केचिद्विलग्ना दशनान्तरेषु
संदृश्यन्ते चूर्णितैरुत्तमाङ्गैः ॥ २७ ॥

Vaktrāṇi te tvara-māṇā viśanti
daṁṣṭrā-karālāni bhayāna-kāni,
kecid-vilagnā daśan-āntareṣu
saṁ-dṛśyante cūrṇitai-rutta-māṅgaiḥ.

वक्त्राणि *vaktrāṇi* = mouths; ते *te* = your; त्वरमाणाः *tvara-māṇāḥ* = hurrying; विशन्ति *viśanti* = enter; दंष्ट्रा-करालानि *daṁṣṭrā-karālāni* = terrible-toothed; भयानकानि *bhayānakāni* = fearful to behold; केचित् *kecit* = some; विलग्नाः *vilagnāḥ* = sticking; दशन-अन्तरेषु *daśana-antareṣu* = in the gaps between the teeth; संदृश्यन्ते *saṁdṛśyante* = are found; चूर्णितैः *cūrṇitaiḥ* = crushed to powder; उत्तम-अङ्गैः *uttama-aṅgaiḥ* = with (their) heads.

27. *Into Your mouths, with terrible teeth, and fearful to behold, they precipitately enter. Some are found sticking in the gaps between the teeth with their heads crushed into powder.*

A philosophy that comprehends the totality without fear or favour and is even true to its mission of seeking Truth, cannot afford to ignore the *destructive*-aspect in nature. No creation is possible without being preceded by the process of destruction of its own existence as the raw material from which the 'created' is produced. On the face of the Universe also, wherever there is "existence" it is nothing but a repetition of constant change, and change can be interpreted either in terms of constant-creation with regard to the *made products*, or as a process of constant-destruction with regard to the *raw-material* that changed.

Thus, we see that in *Hindūism*, the daring Masters of the *Āryan* fold, while extolling the beauty of the Reality, indulged themselves in viewing It not only as the Omniscient-Creator, or as the Omnipotent-Sustainer, but also as the All-powerful Devourer of all names and forms. This may look dreadful to those creeds that have not yet come to watch and analyse Life in its totality.

Arjuna's words are significant. He does not see the Universal-Form itself devouring the names and forms. On the other hand, he observed that all names and forms *"enter in haste into thy mouth."* When we watch an ocean, we do not find the ocean ever rising up to absorb the waves, but the waves which have risen from the ocean, after a momentary play upon the surface, rush back to disappear into the very ocean. The multiplicity that has risen from the Totality, after its play upon the surface of Truth, must necessarily rush back in all hurry into the very Whole from which they had arisen.

Arjuna watches *"all the sons of Dhṛtarāṣṭra, with hosts of kings of earth, Bhīṣma, Droṇa, Karṇa, the son of a charioteer*, along with the warrior chieftains of ours"* entering precipitately into the yawning mouth of the Principle of Destruction in nature. This not only frightens *Arjuna* and unnerves him, but also gives him a confidence to look ahead—in spite of the fact that in numerical strength, in supplies, and in technicians, his own army was much inferior to the mighty forces of the *Kurū-s*. The Vision which he saw, was in fact a peep into the future. In the *Viśvarūpa*, when the Lord expresses Himself as the entire world of phenomena, a conception of oneness arises in which not only space shrinks, but even Time becomes an object-of-observation.

It is no wonder, therefore, that *Arjuna* saw in that picture *the past merging with the present and moving forward to mingle with the entire future*. When I have the entire *Gītā*-book before me, I can read either the preceding two pages or

* *Karṇa*, the son of Lord Sun, born to *Kunti*, is described in *Mahābhārata* as a half-brother to the *Pāṇḍavā-s*. The boy was brought up by a charioteer and some say that his foster-father was the king of *Aṅga* (*Bengal*). *Karṇa* fought on the side of the *Kurū-s* and he was killed in the battle by *Arjuna*.

can skip over them and read the third page ahead or, according to my will and desire, continue reading this very same page. Similarly, when the whole Universe is brought at once within the compass of *Arjuna*'s vision, he could see herein at one gaze "*all the here and the there, and the everywhere*"—so too *the past, the present and the future*. The modern scientists also have now come to realise and accept that Time and Space are one and the same, and they are each expressed in terms of the other.*

The seekers of Truth, themselves truthful, were not at all afraid if their enquiry took them to the aspect of the terrible in the Truth. The world is a combination of the beautiful and the ugly, the good and the bad, the soft and the hard, the sweet and the bitter. God, the Lord, has Himself become all these, and therefore, no adoration of the Lord, or estimate of the Reality, will be complete, if, according to our taste, we recognise only the beautiful, the good, the soft, and the sweet aspects of Him. An unprejudiced and detached mind will have to recognise Him as the ugly and the bad, the hard and the bitter also. That philosophy alone is complete which points out that the Supreme is, in fact, in Its Absolute Nature, beyond all these qualities.

In a purely scientific approach, therefore, *Arjuna* is made to express all the details, even if they be blood-curdling and gruesome. No doubt, the *Gītā* has its own sense of realism. The mouth of death is described here with all faithfulness as "terrible with tusks," "*fearful to behold*."

How do they enter Thy mouth? Arjuna *says:*

यथा नदीनां बहवोऽम्बुवेगाः
समुद्रमेवाभिमुखा द्रवन्ति ।
तथा तवामी नरलोकवीरा
विशन्ति वक्त्राण्यभिविज्वलन्ति ॥ २८ ॥

---

* It is not rarely that we say, 'in the space of an hour.'

Yathā nadīnāṁ bahavo-'mbu-vegāḥ
samudra-mevābhi-mukhā dravanti,
tathā tavāmī nara-loka-vīrā
viśanti vaktrāṇya-bhivi-jvalanti.

यथा *yathā* = as; नदीनाम् *nadīnām* = of rivers; बहवः *bahavaḥ* = many; अम्बु-वेगाः *ambu-vegaḥ* = water currents समुद्रम् *samudram*= to the ocean; एव *eva* = verily; अभिमुखा *abhimukhā* = towards; द्रवन्ति *dravanti* = flow; तथा *tathā* = so; तव *tava* = your; अमी *amī* = these; नर लोक वीराः *nara loka vīrāḥ* = heroes in the world of men; विशन्ति *viśanti* = enter; वक्त्राणि *vaktrāṇi* = mouths; अभि-विज्वलन्ति *abhi-vijvalanti* = flaming

28. *Verily, as many torrents of rivers flow towards the ocean, so these heroes in the world of men enter Your flaming mouths.*

The one great characteristic of the *Āryan* race is that they are, to a point of weakness, essentially poetic in temperament. Whatever be the theme that they handle, if any line of thought tickles the poetry in it, they are incapable of rejecting it. However urgent his mission may be, a true *Hindū* must stop and bend down to enjoy and pat a way side flower nodding in the breeze! He is so acutely aware of the Presence of the Lord everywhere that to him, wherever there is beauty, it is a window through which he can have a peep into the ante chambers of the Truth.*

---

* A story is told about how a famous prostitute, sitting in her balcony noticed that an aged *Sādhu* was standing on the road, gazing at her beautiful form. Lost in admiration, the monk gazed on and the lady getting tired of the state, got up from her seat and retired to her room. But after two hours when she came back to her seat on the balcony, she noticed the same Saint still standing there with his thirsty state. The lady sent her maid inviting the revered old man to her apartment. Receiving the Saint with all respects she enquired why at his sacred age he should so behave as to insult his ochre robe. The answer given by the *Sādhu* is typical of the *Hindū* way-of-thinking. "But" the Saint replied. "It is not at you that I marvel, but, through your beauty, I was adoring the Artist that made it."

Here is a typical example. Revered *Vyāsa*, as he bends down upon his work suddenly gets tickled up by two wondrous pictures that supply in two irreplaceable analogies, the entire picture of the world of names and forms rushing forward only to disappear. In this stanza, the analogy of the torrential rivers, gushing ahead to reach the ocean and become one with it, is used. Each river has, no doubt, its own distinct personality, gathered from the nature and condition of the very terrain through which it has flowed. At no point does any river pause or hesitate to gush forward. An observer of limited powers of understanding may say that each drop of water in its flow in the river is moving towards a known point down on its way; but, to a true observer, all rivers flow towards the ocean and they cannot, and will not, stop until they reach the ocean, having reached which, all distinctions end.

Each drop of water in the river came from the ocean—in the form of a cloud it reached the mountains, and there in the form of rain it manifested; watering the lands on the banks and supplying life and nourishment to the fields, they gushed down in their torrential haste to the very basin from which they took off on this *"Mercy flight."* Similarly, from the Totality, the individuals have come to serve the race, to nourish the culture, to contribute to the beauty of the world...and yet, on their pilgrimage none of them can pause even for a moment en route. All must rush towards the Source from which they arose. The river loses nothing by reaching the ocean. Even though it gathers en route certain special qualities, and therefore, a special name, and has, for itself, a separate tangible form, it is all a temporary phase, a convenience taken up by "the waters of the ocean" to make the dry land smile in plenty.

The more thought is given to it, the more can this stanza yield its secret joys and expose its innate beauty.

Why and how do they enter? Arjuna *says:*

यथा प्रदीप्तं ज्वलनं पतङ्गा
विशन्ति नाशाय समृद्धवेगाः ।
तथैव नाशाय विशन्ति लोकाः
तवापि वक्त्राणि समृद्धवेगाः ॥ २९ ॥

Yathā pradīptaṃ jvalanaṃ pataṅgā
viśanti nāśāya samṛddha-vegāḥ,
tathaiva nāśāya viśanti lokāḥ
tavāpi vaktrāṇi samṛddha-vegāḥ.

यथा *yathā* = as; प्रदीप्तम् *pradīptam* = blazing; ज्वलनम् *jvalanam* = fire; पतङ्गाः *pataṅgāḥ* = moths; विशन्ति *viśanti* = enter; नाशाय *nāśāya* = to destruction; समृद्ध-वेगाः *samṛddha-vegāḥ* = with quickened speed; तथा *tathā* = so; एव *eva* = only; नाशाय *nāśaya* = for destruction; विशन्ति *viśanti* = enter; लोकाः *lokāḥ* = creatures; तव *tava* = your; अपि *api* = also; वक्त्राणि *vaktrāṇi* = mouths; समृद्ध-वेगाः *samṛddha-vegāḥ* = with quickened speed.

29. *As moths rush hurriedly into a blazing fire to their own destruction, so also these creatures hastily rush into Your mouths for their own destruction.*

The essential oneness between the *Manifest* that has come out of the *Unmanifest*, and the very *Unmanifest* which is the womb-of-manifestation, has been beautifully brought out by the picture of the river, which has risen from the ocean and is, in all haste, rushing down only to lose its very name and form, and become one with the ocean.

No analogy can be complete in itself. The picture of the river does not show any intrinsic conscious effort on the part of the river to reach the ocean. The living kingdom, with its own free discrimination, it may be doubted, may not act as the inert waters of the river. To show that even the sentient beings are irresistibly drawn towards the mouth of their own destruction, by the whipping hand of instinct, the example of the "*moths hurriedly rush into a blazing fire to their own destruction*" is given. To *Vyāsa*, the entire nature seems to be an open book-of-scripture, explaining everywhere in all its happenings, the fundamental facts that "the projection of the unmanifest to the manifest-condition is the *process of creation*" and that "the manifest merging back to its own haven of the unmanifest is *destruction or death*." That terrible looking monstrous happening called 'death,' when approached in a correct perspective and with true understanding, unmasks itself to reveal a gladdening face, ever cheerful and gay.

Arjuna's mental tension was mainly created by his hasty evaluation of the enormous destruction he would be causing in the battle-field of *Kurukṣetra. Kṛṣṇa* has to cure him, by lifting him to heights from which he could witness and realise, in one sweeping gaze, the unavoidable phenomenon of death. A close and full understanding of any happening removes the fangs from its threatening hood! It is only when the discriminating intellect of man becomes doped with "ignorance," that the happenings around him can threaten to smother him down. As the river hastens to the ocean, and the moths into the fire, so too all names and forms must, and most irresistibly do, rush towards the unmanifest. With this realisation, anyone can thereafter face life, fearless of death, since life itself becomes to him a process of continuous change.

Therefore death, as a play-of-time, becomes a stingless phenomenon. This is glorified in all its ferocious beauty in the following verses:

लेलिह्यसे ग्रसमानः समन्तात्
लोकान्समग्रान्वदनैर्ज्वलद्भिः ।
तेजोभिरापूर्य जगत्समग्रं
भासस्तवोग्राः प्रतपन्ति विष्णो ॥ ३० ॥

Lelihyase grasa-mānaḥ samantāt
lokān-samagrān-vadanair-jvaladbhiḥ,
tejobhi-rāpūrya jagat-samagraṁ
bhāsas-tavogrāḥ pratapanti viṣṇo.

लेलिह्यसे *lelihyase* = you lick; ग्रसमानः *grasamānaḥ* = devouring; समन्तात् *samantāt* = on every side; लोकान् *lokān* = the worlds; समग्रान् *samagrān* = all; वदनैः *vadanaiḥ* = with mouths; ज्वलद्भिः *jvaladbhiḥ* = flaming; तेजोभिः *tejobhiḥ* = with radiance; आपूर्य *āpūrya* = filling; जगत् *jagat* = the world; समग्रम् *samagram* = the whole; भासः *bhāsaḥ* = rays; तव *tava* = your; उग्राः *ugrāḥ* = fierce; प्रतपन्ति *pratapanti* = are burning; विष्णो *viṣṇo* = O Viṣṇu.

30. Devouring all worlds on every side with Your flaming mouths, You are licking (in enjoyment). Your fierce rays, filling the whole world with radiance, are burning, O Viṣṇu.

After composing some surging poetry, *Vyāsa* faithfully comes back to the line of thought he was developing earlier. Hosts of men and things of the world reach the Mouth to perish therein. The hungry 'Mouth' is never tired, for, the Principle of Destruction has a never-ending appetite, and after "*devouring all worlds with Your flaming mouths You are licking (in enjoyment),*" exclaims *Arjuna*.

In fact, the stanza clearly brings forth the implication underlying the concept of the Trinity. The Creator, the Sustainer, and the Destroyer are three distinct entities in concept, but in their actual workings, they constitute a simultaneous process. Creation is continued in a chain of destruction, and the process of destruction is not a total annihilation but only a change from one form to another, thereby ending in a new Creation. "Constructive destruction" is the secret philosophy behind the continuity of Existence observed everywhere.

In a cinema show, various poses on the film are made to run on in front of the arc-light, and each picture that has passed away from the arc-light may be considered as dead, and those reaching the arc-light as those that are born. The continuity in these two series of happenings of births and deaths, or constructions and destructions, gives us the hallucination of a logical sequence in the theme revealed on the screen. Conditioned by 'place and time,' things and beings, happenings and circumstances, come and go in the plane of our experiences and their continuity is what we experience as "existence."

The above idea can be repeated in the language of our traditional belief in the Trinity. *Brahmājī*, the Creator, cannot create unless *Śiva*, the Destroyer, is functioning simultaneously on the same anvil. And *Viṣṇu*, the Sustainer, will never come to play unless the Creator and the Destroyer work feverishly and consistently. The whole world of multiplicity is thus an expression of *Viṣṇu*, the Sustainer, which is nothing other than the product of the game played by both the Creator and the Destroyer!

When, with such depth of understanding, *Arjuna* looks at the mighty resplendence of the Totality-Form, he feels almost blindfolded by "*fierce rays filling the whole world* with radiance."

You are fearsome, therefore:

आख्याहि मे को भवानुग्ररूपो
नमोऽस्तु ते देववर प्रसीद ।
विज्ञातुमिच्छामि भवन्तमाद्यं
न हि प्रजानामि तव प्रवृत्तिम् ॥ ३१ ॥

Ākhyāhi me ko bhavān-ugra-rūpo
namo-'stu te deva-vara prasīda,
vijñātum-icchāmi bhavantam-ādyaṁ
na hi prajānāmi tava pravṛttim.

आख्याहि *ākhyāhi* = tell; मे *me* = me; कः *kaḥ* = who (are); भवान् *bhavān* = you; उग्ररूपः *ugra-rūpaḥ* = fierce in form; नमः *namaḥ* = salutations; अस्तु *astu* = be; ते *te* = to you; देववर *deva-vara* = O God Supreme; प्रसीद *prasīda* = have mercy; विज्ञातुम् *vijñātum* = to know; इच्छामि *icchāmi* = (I) wish; भवन्तम् *bhavantam* = you; आद्यम् *ādyam* = the original being; न *na* = not; हि *hi* = indeed; प्रजानामि *prajānāmi* = (I) know; तव *tava* = your; प्रवृत्तिम् *pravṛttim* = purpose, doing.

31. *Tell me, who You are, so fierce in form? Salutations to You, O God Supreme; have mercy. I desire to know You, the Original Being (Primeval One), I know not indeed Your purpose.*

Arjuna realises suddenly the sanctity and the divinity of the Lord's Power, and so, in an inspired rush of veneration, he bows down to Him whom till now he took to be but a cowherd boy of *Vṛṁdāvana*. Intellectual though he may be, here is an experience too big for him to observe fully, analyse carefully, and digest completely. The only thing he can do is to surrender himself at the very feet of the Lord, requesting Him, "*Tell me who You are*?"

To reinforce the solidity of the query, *Arjuna* indicates that his question deserves an answer, for, "*I desire to know You, O Primeval One.*" It is very well-known in the textbooks of spirituality, that "a burning aspiration to know" is the motive force behind every seeker's mind and intellect. But here *Arjuna* is preoccupied with the problem of challenge that is facing him, and therefore, he is not, in fact, directly seeking the Divine Truth behind the Vision. His enquiry is highly coloured by the emotion of fear in him and his anxiety to know what would be the outcome of the war. This is clear from the last line wherein he himself explains: "*I know not indeed Your purpose*!" The enquiry made here is "What is the mission of the Lord in taking such a terrible form, and in presenting Himself in front of *Arjuna*, exhibiting how the *Kaurava* forces are marching in all hurry towards the burning Mouth-of-Death?" When he intensely longs for a thing to happen and when sure signs, forecasting his success, present themselves, he needs a confirmation from others. Here *Arjuna* is witnessing what he exactly wishes should happen. But the Prince wants to get a confirmation of the same from *Kṛṣṇa* Himself. Hence this question.

Introducing Himself as the manifestation of Truth in its aspect of destruction, the Lord in the Universal Form declares:

श्रीभगवानुवाच-

कालोऽस्मि लोकक्षयकृत्प्रवृद्धो
लोकान्समाहर्तुमिह प्रवृत्तः ।
ऋतेऽपि त्वां न भविष्यन्ति सर्वे
येऽवस्थिताः प्रत्यनीकेषु योधाः ॥ ३२ ॥

Śrī Bhagavān Uvāca,
Kālo-'smi loka-kṣaya-kṛt-pravṛddho
lokān-samāhartum-iha pravṛttaḥ,
ṛte-'pi tvām na bhaviṣyanti sarve
ye'vasthitāḥ pratya-nīkeṣu yodhāḥ.

कालः *kālaḥ* = time; अस्मि *asmi* = (I) am; लोक-क्षय-कृत् *loka-kṣaya-kṛt* = world destroying; प्रवृद्धः *pravṛddhaḥ* = mighty; लोकान् *lokān* = the worlds; समाहर्तुम् *samāhartum* = to destroy; इह *iha* = here; प्रवृत्तः *pravṛttaḥ* = engaged; ऋते *ṛte* = without; अपि *api* = also; त्वाम् *tvām* = you; न *na* = not; भविष्यन्ति *bhaviṣyanti* = shall live; सर्वे *sarve* = all; ये *ye* = these; अवस्थिताः *avasthitāḥ* = arrayed; प्रति-अनीकेषु *prati-anīkeṣu* = in hostile armies; योधाः *yodhāḥ* = warriors.

The Blessed Lord said:

32. I am the mighty world-destroying Time, now engaged in destroying the worlds. Even without

You, none of the warriors arrayed in hostile armies shall live.

No construction of any thing is possible without a corresponding destruction of its own previous condition. The world is created by a continuous process of destruction. Today has arisen from the graves of yesterday. Childhood dies before youth appears. And when youth passes away, old age takes its birth. The power visibly playing behind constructive destruction is the fundamental Power that rules over and governs the life of beings. *Kṛṣṇa* introduces Himself here as "*I am the mighty world-destroying Time*," who has manifested to wipe out the generation that has suffered decay in its own false sense-of-values and wrong assumptions about life and its purpose.

The world-destroying attitude of the Lord is not at all against His all-merciful concept. Sometimes there is mercy in destruction. A broken bridge, a dilapidated dam, and an ancient building are instances in point. To pull them down is the most merciful act of charity that any considerate government can do to the community; so too here.

By declaring that the very purpose behind this manifestation is to destroy totally the negative forces that strangle the cultural life of the country, *Kṛṣṇa* is confirming *Arjuna*'s vague hope that there is yet a chance of victory for his army. Reassuring the very same idea, the Universal-Form here declares that in the great mission of reconstruction, the Lord is not depending upon any individual or individuals. It is 'Time' that is going to bring the renaissance and achieve the revival. In such a colossal movement of universal rehabilitation, individuals are but mere creatures of destiny. In spite of them, and with or without their co-operation, Time's plans will be worked out. The country needs the revival; the world demands man's rehabilitation. *Kṛṣṇa* clearly says, "*Even without you*" none of the warriors manning the secular folly of sheer materialism shall survive the war of the imminent cultural upheaval.

In the context of the *Mahābhārata* story, it almost amounts to saying that the *Kaurava* forces have all been killed already by Time, and that *Arjuna*, by co-operating and serving the Army of Renaissance, is only backing the sure success.

Therefore, as a representative man of all times, Arjuna*, is advised to perform fearless action in life:*

तस्मात्त्वमुत्तिष्ठ यशो लभस्व
जित्वा शत्रून् भुङ्क्ष्व राज्यं समृद्धम् ।
मयैवैते निहताः पूर्वमेव
निमित्तमात्रं भव सव्यसाचिन् ॥ ३३ ॥

Tasmāt-tvam-uttiṣṭha yaśo labhasva
jitvā śatrūn bhuṅkṣva rājyaṁ samṛddham,
mayai-vaite nihatāḥ pūrva-meva
nimitta-mātraṁ bhava savya-sācin.

तस्मात् *tasmāt* = therefore; त्वम् *tvam* = you; उत्तिष्ठ *uttiṣṭha* = stand up; यशः *yaśaḥ* = fame; लभस्व *labhasva* = obtain; जित्वा *jitvā* = having conquered; शत्रून् *śatrūn* = enemies; भुङ्क्ष्व *bhuṅkṣva* = enjoy; राज्यम् *rājyam* = the kingdom; समृद्धम् *samṛddham* = the flourishing; मया *mayā* = by Me; एव *eva* = even; एते *ete* = these; निहताः *nihatāḥ* = have been slain; पूर्वम् *pūrvam* = already; एव *eva* = even; निमित्त-मात्रम् *nimitta-mātram* = a mere instrument; भव *bhava* = be; सव्यसाचिन् *savyasācin* = O left-handed one.

33. *Therefore, stand up, and obtain fame. Conquer the enemies and enjoy the flourishing kingdom. Verily by Myself they have already been slain; be you a mere instrument, O left-handed archer.*

द्रोणं च भीष्मं च जयद्रथं च
कर्णं तथान्यानपि योधवीरान् ।
मया हतांस्त्वं जहि मा व्यथिष्ठा
युध्यस्व जेतासि रणे सपत्नान् ॥ ३४ ॥

Droṇaṁ ca bhīṣmaṁ ca jayadrathaṁ ca
karṇaṁ tathā-nyānapi yodha-vīrān,
mayā hatāṁs-tvaṁ jahi mā vyathiṣṭhā
yudhyasva jetāsi raṇe sapatnān.

द्रोणम् *droṇam* = *Droṇa*; च *ca* = and; भीष्मम् *bhīṣmam* = *Bhīṣma*; च *ca* = and; जयद्रथम् *jayadratham* = *Jayadratha*; च *ca* = and; कर्णम् *karṇam* = *Karṇa*; तथा *tathā* = also; अन्यान् *anyān* = others; अपि *api* = also; योध-वीरान् *yodha-vīrān* = brave warriors; मया *mayā* = by me; हतान् *hatān* = slain; त्वम् *tvam* = you; जहि *jahi* = do kill; मा *mā* = not; व्यथिष्ठा: *vyathiṣṭhāḥ* = be distressed with fear; युध्यस्व *yudhyasva* = fight; जेतासि *jetāsi* = shall conquer; रणे *raṇe* = in the battle; सपत्नान् *sapatnān* = the enemies.

34. Droṇa, Bhīṣma, Jayadratha, Karṇa, *and other brave warriors—those have already been slain by Me; you do kill; be not distressed with fear; fight and you shall conquer your enemies in battle.*

Here Lord *Kṛṣṇa* is very directly consoling *Arjuna* that he should stand up and catch the Time and claim success and glory. Whatever be the might and strength of the negative forces, the all-consuming Might-of-Change has already destroyed them all, and *Arjuna* has only to come forward, act the part of a hero and claim the crown of victory all to himself: "*Verily by Myself they have already been slain, be you a mere instrument, O left-handed archer.*"

In fact, to every thinking man, the truth is obvious that in life, he is at best only an instrument in His hands. We are not generally ready to accept this proposition, because, the self-arrogating ego-sense in us will not easily retire so as to allow the Divine in us to play out in all its omnipotence. Everywhere, in all our activities, when we analyse each one of our actions, we find that our actual contribution in them all is a meagre share, compared to what nature has supplied, and what the unseen hand has achieved for us. At best, we can only combine things that already exist, and coax out of their own natural qualities and properties, a certain result, and then claim vainly that we have created something new.

The radio, the aeroplane, the roaring engines, the subtle machinery, the wonder-drugs, in short, the entire "Brave New World," and all its achievements in progress—are all nothing but the play of children in the lap of the Lord who, in fact, is the One who has ordered and allowed us to have electricity, iron, ether, air, etc., with their special properties. Without these, no achievement is ever possible; and achievements are nothing but intelligent acts of the assembling and re-assembling of these very God-given things.

Two jugs, one containing some hot water and the other some cold water, are placed by the mother of a child and the child mixes them and gets the required lukewarm water. If the little one boasts that he has created or made it, the mother, in all her instinctive kindness, may, no doubt, congratulate the child but she knows what the reality is!

The concept of self-surrender and the theory of serving the world in constant awareness of the Lord, are not idle dreams prescribed for escaping the gross realities of the world. It is essential for man to raise his calibre and temper so as to work efficiently and achieve success in the world. It is the technique of keeping oneself constantly in a mood of tireless enthusiasm and joyous inspiration.

The world is too much with the ego. To the extent the ego is surrendered in the awareness of the greater and the nobler, to that extent, the entire world and achievements therein become a game of simple and sure success everywhere. Earlier in the *Gītā*, it was, at many points, strictly pointed out that through the technique of self-surrender, the greater possibilities can be milked out of us. The same idea is again repeated here. The entire army has been invited here only to play the part of the hero—serve as His Instruments and let them claim for themselves the crown and the glory as their wages.

Arjuna had certain reasons why he should be particularly afraid of some of the top men in the *Kaurava* forces. They are taken up one by one and the Lord indicates how even they have already been killed by the All-consuming Time-Spirit.

Droṇa was *Arjuna*'s teacher who taught him the art of archery. The *Ācārya* had with him some special weapons and he was particularly revered and respected by *Arjuna*. The grandsire *Bhīṣma* had his death at his command, and he too had very powerful celestial weapons. Once in the past *Bhīṣma* had made *Paraśurāma* lick the ground.

Jayadratha was invincible; for, his father who was engaged in *tapas*, had firmly resolved that "whoever causes my son's head to drop down on earth, his head too shall fall." *Karṇa* also had a powerful missile given to him by *Indra*.

It becomes clear now why these four names are particularly enumerated by the Lord in the list of personalities that Time had already devastated. Even these great warriors have been eliminated by the Principle-of-Destruction, and thereby, it has been brought home to *Arjuna* that the field is clear for him to play his part and advance towards the throne and crown, and claim the entire glory as his own.

It is natural that, when a burning desire in an individual is fulfilled, he suddenly bursts into an irresistible glorification of his kindly patron:

सञ्जय उवाच-
एतच्छ्रुत्वा वचनं केशवस्य
कृताञ्जलिर्वेपमानः किरीटी ।
नमस्कृत्वा भूय एवाह कृष्णं
सगद्गदं भीतभीतः प्रणम्य ॥ ३५ ॥

Sañjaya Uvāca—

Etac-chrutvā vacanaṁ keśavasya
kṛtāñjalir-vepamānaḥ kirīṭī,
namas-kṛtvā bhūya evāha kṛṣṇaṁ
sagad-gadaṁ bhīta-bhītaḥ praṇamya.

एतत् *etat* = that; श्रुत्वा *śrutvā* = having heard; वचनम् *vacanam* = speech; केशवस्य *keśavasya* = of *Keśava*; कृताञ्जलिः *kṛtāñjaliḥ* = with joined palms; वेपमानः *vepamānaḥ* = trembling; किरीटी *kirīṭī* = the crowned-one; नमस्कृत्वा *namaskṛtvā* = prostrating (himself); भूयः *bhūyaḥ* = again; एव *eva* = even; आह *āha* = addressed; कृष्णम् *kṛṣṇam* = to *Kṛṣṇa*; सगद्-गदम् *sagad-gadam* = in a choked voice; भीतभीतः *bhīta-bhītaḥ* = overwhelmed with fear; प्रणम्य *praṇamya* = having prostrated.

Sañjaya said:

35. *Having heard that speech of* Keśava (Kṛṣṇa), *the crowned-one* (Arjuna), *with joined palms, trembling and prostrating himself, again addressed* Kṛṣṇa, *in a choked voice, bowing down, overwhelmed with fear.*

The dramatist in *Vyāsa*, with his innate craftsmanship, lifts the scene from the battle front to the quiet and silent chambers of the palace, where the blind *Dhṛtarāṣṭra* is listening to 'the running commentary' given by *Sañjaya*. In thus lifting the reader more than once* away from the awe-inspiring atmosphere of *Kurukṣetra*, *Vyāsa* is not only adding dynamic movement to the

* In this very chapter, we are taken three times to the palace and back again to the battle-field.

picture but also giving a necessary psychological rest for the reader's mind from such a subtle theme of awful beauty.

It is not to be forgotten at all that *Sañjaya* in the *Gītā* is "*Our own special correspondent,*" who is fully sympathetic with the righteous cause of the *Pāṇḍavā*-s. Naturally, therefore, as soon as he reports the Lord's own words—that all the mighty men of the times, who are the top-ranking men in position in the *Kaurava* forces, have already been annihilated—he wants to bring to the blind old man's awareness, the magnitude of the impending disaster. As we have noticed earlier, the only one who could call the war off, even at this moment, is *Dhṛtarāṣṭra* himself. And *Sañjaya* is very anxious to see that the war is not fought. Thus, we see here, in the stanza, in the very language used, the motive of the reporter.

Having heard that speech of Keśava (Kṛṣṇa), the crowned-one (Arjuna), with joined palms, trembling and prostrating himself, again addressed :—The very language used and the picture drawn, reflects the mind of the reporter. Suddenly, *Arjuna* is called here as "the crowned-one," perhaps, as a bold forecast, by which *Sañjaya* expects *Dhṛtarāṣṭra* to see the folly of the disastrous war. But a blind man can never *see* things, and much less if he is intellectually blind with delusion.

If the good sense of the blind king cannot be invoked because of his extremely deluded love for his children, *Sañjaya* expects to give a psychological treatment to the royal father. A lengthy description of how others are getting frightened is a sure method of spreading panic even among moderately courageous listeners. If *Arjuna*, the warrior, the bosom friend of *Kṛṣṇa* is "*trembling and prostrating himself in a choked voice, bowing down, over-whelmed with fear addressed the Lord,*" *Sañjaya* expects every sensible man to realise the horrors of the war that is imminent, and the dire consequences that are in store for the vanquished. Even these words of *Sañjaya* have no effect upon *Dhṛtarāṣṭra* who is blind to everything except his mad affection for his own children.

Arjuna *apostrophizes the universal-form:*

अर्जुन उवाच-

स्थाने हृषीकेश तव प्रकीर्त्या
जगत्प्रहृष्यत्यनुरज्यते च ।
रक्षांसि भीतानि दिशो द्रवन्ति
सर्वे नमस्यन्ति च सिद्धसंघाः ॥ ३६ ॥

Arjuna uvāca—
Sthāne hṛṣīkeśa tava prakīrtyā
jagat-prahṛṣya-tyanu-rajyate ca,
rakṣāṁsi bhītāni diśo dravanti
sarve namasyanti ca siddha-saṁghāḥ.

स्थाने *sthāne* = it is meet (fitting, just right); हृषीकेश *hṛṣīkeśa* = O *Hṛṣīkeśa*; तव *tava* = thy; प्रकीर्त्या *prakīrtyā* = in praise; जगत् *jagat* = the world; प्रहृष्यति *prahṛṣyati* = is delighted; अनुरज्यते *anurajyate* = rejoices; च *ca* = and; रक्षांसि *rakṣāṁsi* = the *Rākṣasā-s*; भीतानि *bhītāni* = in fear; दिशः *diśaḥ* = to all quarters; द्रवन्ति *dravanti* = fly; सर्वे *sarve* = all; नमस्यन्ति *namasyanti* = bow (to thee); च *ca* = and; सिद्ध-संघाः *siddha-saṁghāḥ* = the hosts of *Siddhā-s.*

Arjuna said:

36. *It is but meet, O* Hṛṣīkeśa *(*Kṛṣṇa*), that the world delights and rejoices in Thy praise;* Rākṣasā-s *fly in fear to all quarters, and all hosts of* Siddhā-s *bow to Thee.*

Again from the luxurious chambers of riches and splendour, the students of the *Gītā* are lifted, on the lyrical charm of the poem, to the humming ground of the battle-field and to the Wonder-Form of the Lord. The picture of *Arjuna* addressing the Lord with his hands folded, trembling with fear, singing songs of adoration, with a throat chocked with fear and wonderment is effectively drawn. This passage, containing the following *eleven* stanzas, represents one of the most beautiful prayers that we have in *Hindūism.* In fact, the words and the ideas expressed hereunder are so general in their import and significance that we can almost say that no better Universal Prayer can ever be conceived of, either in its concept, beauty, or cadence, or in the depth of the message in its words.

In these passages, the cognising power in *Arjuna* is steadily realising the diviner Truth behind the details of that Total-Form. When one watches and sees one's own reflection in a mirror, it is rarely that the observer sees the mirror-surface. When one watches the surface of the mirror, the reflection is either not at all available or, at best is only dimly recognised.

So long as *Arjuna* is preoccupied with the details of the Universal-Form, he does not realise, or recognise, the Infinite which is the very core of the *Viśvarūpa.* In these passages, it is evident that *Arjuna* has started sensing the deeper meaning that lies behind the cosmic wonder represented to him in his vision Divine.

In the stanza under discussion, *Hṛṣīkeśa* can be interpreted as "*one with short-clipped hair*"[1] or as "*the Lord of the Senses.*"[2] In the former case, *Arjuna* is addressing *Kṛṣṇa,* the Universal Form with Its hairs close-clipped or in the latter meaning, which no doubt is more appropriate with what is to follow, he is addressing the Self, the Lord of the Senses. The rest of the lines become quite clear when the term *Hṛṣīkeśa* is understood as the Self.

The Self is the theme of all invocations, in everyone, in all actions and thoughts. To the extent the Self is revealed and asserted, to that extent animalism, constituting the *Rākṣasik*-forces, must depart. And the good will, naturally, be inspired to bow down in reverence to the Vision of the Self.

Why should they bow down?

---

1. *Hṛṣī* (curled up or standing on end) + *keśa* (locks, hairs) = *Hṛṣīkeśa*—Curled up locks or close cropped.
2. *Hṛṣīka* (an organ of sense) + *Īśa* (Lord) = *Hṛṣīkeśa*—Lord of the Senses.

कस्माच्च ते न नमेरन्महात्मन्
गरीयसे ब्रह्मणोऽप्यादिकर्त्रे ।
अनन्त देवेश जगन्निवास
त्वमक्षरं सदसत्तत्परं यत् ॥ ३७ ॥

Kasmāc-ca te na nameran-mahātman
garīyase brahmaṇo-'pyādi-kartre,
ananta deveśa jagan-nivāsa
tvam-akṣaraṁ sad-asat-tat-paraṁ yat.

कस्मात् *kasmāt* = why; च *ca* = and; ते *te* = they; न *na* = not; नमेरन् *nameran* = may prostrate; महात्मन् *mahātman* = O great-souled one; गरीयसे *garīyase* = greater; ब्रह्मण: *brahmaṇaḥ* = of *Brahmā*; अपि *api* = also; आदि कर्त्रे *ādi kartre* = the primal cause; अनन्त *ananta* = Infinite Being; देवेश *deveśa* = Lord of Lords; जगन्निवास *jagannivāsa* = abode of the Universe; त्वम् *tvam* = your; अक्षरम् *akṣaram* = imperishable; सत् *sat* = the being, manifest; असत् *asat* = non-being, un-manifest; तत् *tat* = that; परम् *param* = the Supreme; यत् *yat* = which.

37. *And why should they not, O Great-souled One, bow to Thee, greater (than all else), the Primal Cause even of* Brahmā, *O Infinite Being, O Lord of Lords, O Abode of the Universe, You are the Imperishable, that which is beyond both the Manifest and the Unmanifest.*

Explaining why the great men of knowledge and wisdom also cannot but prostrate at the Lord's feet, *Arjuna* tries to indicate here the majesty and divinity of the Lord in his Infinite Nature.

Why should they not bow down to Thee, O Great-souled One:—Because the Lord as the Primal Cause of even the Creator, who creates the entire universe of multiplicity, is like the mud in all mud-pots, or the gold in all gold ornaments. The ornaments or the pots have no existence at all apart from the gold-essence or the mud-essence in them. Thus, the Primal Cause is that which pervades everything and is that which holds together all names and forms. Infinite in nature, the Lord is not only the Universe, but he is the Lord of all Lords, inasmuch as even the denizens of the heavens and the great phenomenal powers—all derive their individual might from the Source of all Powers, this Infinite Truth.

The entire world of things-and-beings that exist, can fall under two categories: the Manifest (*sat*) and the Unmanifest (*asat*). The manifest is that which can become objects of experience for the organs-of-perception, for the instrument-of-feeling and the equipment-of-thought. The Unmanifest is that which causes the perceptions, feelings, and thoughts. These subtle causes that order the individuals to live in the world outside, are called *vāsanā-s* and these constitute the Unmanifest. *Arjuna*'s beautiful definition of the Lord accepts that the Lord is not only the Manifest (*sat*), but the Unmanifest (*asat*) as well. And He is also that which transcends them both.

That which is beyond both the Manifest and the Unmanifest:—In the theatre we can enjoy both tragedy and comedy, but the light that illumines the stage is that which transcends them both. The wedding-ring is, no doubt, made of gold; the wedding-necklace is also, no doubt, made of gold; but gold cannot be defined as the necklace or the ring. We will have to say that gold is not only the ring or the necklace but also that which transcends them both. In this sense, the Lord, being the essential Truth in all names and forms, is both the Manifest and the Unmanifest, and He also has a status that transcends both these conditions. In fact, that which makes both the Manifest and the Unmanifest possible is the Light of Awareness, the Pure Consciousness, the Universal Lord, whom *Arjuna* is invoking here.

These few stanzas (36 to 44) represent the most universal prayer that we have in all the religious literature of the world. There cannot be any creed or caste which has any objection to these, in as much as they summarise the entire galaxy of philosophic thoughts regarding the eternal, and expand with them the devotee's heart which can reach dimensions almost unknowable, yet within a devotee's experience.

Arjuna *extols the Lord thus*:

त्वमादिदेवः पुरुषः पुराणः
त्वमस्य विश्वस्य परं निधानम् ।
वेत्तासि वेद्यं च परं च धाम
त्वया ततं विश्वमनन्तरूप ॥ ३८ ॥

Tvamādi-devaḥ puruṣaḥ purāṇaḥ
tvamasya viśvasya paraṁ nidhānam,
vettāsi vedyaṁ ca paraṁ ca dhāma
tvayā tataṁ viśva-mananta-rūpa.

त्वम् *tvam* = you; आदि-देवः *ādi-devaḥ* = the Primal God; पुरुषः *puruṣaḥ* = *Puruṣa*; पुराणः *purāṇaḥ* = the ancient; त्वम् *tvam* = you; अस्य *asya* = of this; विश्वस्य *viśvasya* = of Universe; परम् *param* = the Supreme; निधानम् *nidhānam* = refuge; वेत्ता *vettā* = knower; असि *asi* = (you) are; वेद्यम् *vedyam* = to be known; च *ca* = and; परम् *param* = the Supreme; च *ca* = and; धाम *dhāma* = abode; त्वया *tvayā* = by thee; ततम् *tatam* = is pervaded; विश्वम् *viśvam* = the Universe; अनन्त-रूप *ananta-rūpa* = O Being of infinite forms.

38. *You are the Primal God, the Ancient* Puruṣa *; You are the Supreme Refuge of this Universe. You are the knower, the knowable, and the Abode-Supreme. By Thee is the Universe pervaded, O Being of Infinite forms.*

Continuing in the same strain, *Arjuna* indicates that he considers *Kṛṣṇa* not merely as *Śrī Gopāla Nandana* or merely as *Śrī Vāsudeva*, but as the very Essence upon which the pluralistic world has been built up. This stanza lends a charm that is almost compelling.

You are the Primal God, the Ancient Puruṣa:—The Self is the Supreme Creator. The Pure Consciousness is the womb from which even the Creator has risen. The Self, conditioned by Its own creative urge, plays the part of the Creator.

You are the Supreme Refuge and the Abode-supreme of this Universe:—The entire *Viśva* is housed in the Lord, and therefore, it is said that the Lord is the Abode for the Universe. Here, the term *Viśva* is to be correctly understood. When this is translated as the "Universe," we are apt to confuse it with the astronomers' universe or the scientists' universe. The *Saṁskṛta* term *Viśva* includes these and even more. It includes the entire world of perceptions and the whole field of emotions and the total realms of thought that we, as intelligent individuals, experience in all our lives. This totality of the world of experiences through the body, mind and intellect together is indicated by the term *Viśva*.

With this understanding of the term *Viśva*, it should not be very difficult for the students of *Vedānta* to understand the full meaning of this life. We are all now experiencing our world through the *matter* equipments of our body, mind and intellect. These, being products of inert *matter*, have no Consciousness of their own except that which they borrow from the Infinite, the Self.

These *matter* envelopments, we have already indicated, are not produced from the Self, as the Self is changeless. The *world of matter* cannot be said to arise from any other independent source, since the Self is All-pervading and is the One-without-a-second. Therefore, it is explained that the *Viśva* is but a super-imposition upon the Truth, as the *ghost*-vision gained on a *post*. In all such hallucinations, the *post* is the abode of the *ghost*, of the emotions which it creates, and of the thoughts it generates. There is no truth in the *ghost* apart from the *post* from which it borrows its *ghost-form*. Thus, it is the Self that is indicated here by *Arjuna* when he so beautifully sings that the Lord is the "Supreme Abode" of the entire *Viśva*.

You are the knower and the knowable—The Awareness in us is the Factor that completes all our experiences as realities. If the Light of Awareness were not to illumine the inert world-of-matter, no knowledge would have been possible, and therefore, the Principle of Consciousness, represented here as Lord *Kṛṣṇa*, the Charioteer—is described here as the Knower. All the techniques of Self-realisation are methods of gathering our Consciousness from all its channels of dissipation, so that, in the still moments of thoughtless Awareness, the Self is automatically *recognised*. It is thus said 'the Knowable,' or the realisable.

By Thee is the Universe (of forms pervaded):—Just as sweetness pervades all chocolates, as the ocean pervades all waves, the Lord, being the essence, pervades everything. It was said just a little before, that the super-impositions cannot exist apart from the Substratum upon which they are being perceived. The Self is the Substratum on which the multitude of the world-of-plurality is visualised, and therefore, it is rightly said that "*He pervades all.*" This is only a repetition of the great *Upaniṣadik* Truth that "the Infinite pervades all, and nothing pervades It."

No better definition can be so beautifully couched in a mellifluous language as is done in this stanza. Poetic genius married to philosophy and living together at the house of Ecstasy is *Gītā*. And these are stanzas wherein *Arjuna* forgets his own limitations and expresses, in and through himself, some deeper experiences that he seems to have gained, all of a sudden.

वायुर्यमोऽग्निर्वरुणः शशाङ्कः
प्रजापतिस्त्वं प्रपितामहश्च ।
नमो नमस्तेऽस्तु सहस्त्रकृत्वः
पुनश्च भूयोऽपि नमो नमस्ते ॥ ३९ ॥

Vāyur-yamo-'gnir-varuṇaḥ śaśāṅkaḥ
prajāpatis-tvaṁ pra-pitāmahaś-ca,
namo namaste-'stu sahasra-kṛtvaḥ
punaś-ca bhūyo-'pi namo namaste.

वायु: *vāyuḥ* = *Vāyu*; यम: *yamaḥ* = *Yama*; अग्नि: *agniḥ* = fire; वरुण: *varuṇaḥ* = *Varuṇa*; शशाङ्क: *śaśāṅkaḥ* = Moon; प्रजापति: *prajāpatiḥ* = *Prājapati*; त्वम् *tvam* = thou; प्रपितामह: *pra-pitāmahaḥ* = great grandfather; च *ca* = and; नम: *namaḥ* = salutations; नम: *namaḥ* = salutations; ते *te* = to you; अस्तु *astu* = be; सहस्र-कृत्व: *sahasra-kṛtvaḥ* = thousand times; पुन: *punaḥ* = again; च *ca* = and; भूय: *bhūyaḥ* = again; अपि *api* = also; नम: *namaḥ* = salutations; नम: *namaḥ* = salutations; ते *te* = to you.

39. You are Vāyu, Yama, Agni, Varuṇa, *the Moon,* Prajāpati, *and the great-grandfather (of all). Salutations! Salutations unto You a thousand times, and again salutations unto You!*

So far *Arjuna* was chanting the glories of the God in His transcendental form. A devotee (*Upāsaka*) may wonder what exactly the relationship of the Supreme with his particular Lord-of-the-heart (*Upāsya*) is. The forms and names of *Deities* conceived of, and fervently prayed to, in ancient times, are generally representations of the manifested phenomenal powers.

In the *Vedik* period, *Vāyu* (the Wind), *Yama* (the Destroyer), *Agni* (the Fire), *Varuṇa* (the Sea-god), *Śaśāṅka* (the Moon)* and *Prajāpati* (the Creator) were considered as *Deities* for reverence and devotion, concentration and growth of the seeker's inner personality. These gods were invoked in those days through chantings and worship, through rituals and sacrifices, and therefore, they were the only popular concepts of God even in the minds of the educated. Often times and everywhere, "means" have a tendency to get misunderstood as the very "goal." *Arjuna*, here in his true understanding, indicates the Infinite, the Source of all potentialities, the Lord, as nothing other than *Kṛṣṇa*, the Infinite.

That the Supreme Lord, in fact, expressing through various functions, Himself plays the part of these *Deities*, is an acceptable view from the standpoint of *Vedānta*. In our own

* *Śaśāṅka* (the moon) : Literally it means the 'hare marked' indicating the rabbit-like form that is seen as a patch on the moon's face.

times it is usual for the devotees to invoke the Lord and assert that 'the Lord of their heart' is the Lord of all Lords. To this Lord of all Lords, *Arjuna* prostrates.

"And........................."

नमः पुरस्तादथ पृष्ठतस्ते
नमोऽस्तु ते सर्वत एव सर्व ।
अनन्तवीर्यामितविक्रमस्त्वं
सर्वं समाप्नोषि ततोऽसि सर्वः ॥ ४० ॥

Namaḥ purastād-atha pṛṣṭha-taste
namo-'stu te sarvata eva sarva,
ananta-vīryāmita-vikramas-tvaṁ
sarvaṁ samāpnoṣi tato-'si sarvaḥ.

नमः *namaḥ* = salutations; पुरस्तात् *purastāt* = (from) before; अथ *atha* = also; पृष्ठतः *pṛṣṭhataḥ* = (from) behind; ते *te* = to you; नमः *namaḥ* = salutations; अस्तु *astu* = be; ते *te* = to you; सर्वतः *sarvataḥ* = on every side; एव *eva* = even; सर्व *sarva* = all; अनन्त-वीर्य. *ananta-vīrya* = infinite in power; अमित-विक्रमः *āmita-vikramaḥ* = infinite in prowess (inmeasurable in strength); त्वम् *tvam* = you; सर्वम् *sarvam* = all; समाप्नोषि *samāpnoṣi* = pervade; ततः *tataḥ* = wherefore, and therefore; असि *asi* = (you) are; सर्वः *sarvaḥ* = all.

40. *Salutations to You, before and behind! Salutations to You on every side! O All! You, Infinite in Power, and Infinite in Prowess, You pervade all; wherefore You are the All.*

The Supreme dwells everywhere within, without, above, below and around, and there is no place where He is not.* This

* The same idea is expressed in *Muṇḍaka Upaniṣad* II-2. : Luminous, subtler than the subtlest, imperishable *Brahman* is the abode of the world and all its inhabitants. He is Life, Speech, Mind, Reality, Immortality. That is the mark which should be penetrated by the mind. Penetrate it. Oh my Friend." Also the same idea more or less is expressed in *Chāndogya Upaniṣad* : VII-25.

is not an original idea at all. This has been the constant state of actual experience of all the great *Ṛṣī-s* of the *Upaniṣad-s*.

The Lord, to whom *Arjuna* thus mentally prostrates from all sides, is not only the All-pervading Essence like space in the Universe, but is also the "womb" from which all power and daring flow out. Wherever there is an incentive to act, or a capacity to achieve, it is all a ray of His infinite potentiality. The Supreme as Pure Existence dwells everywhere, in everything and in all beings. Since nothing can exist without Existence, He, as Pure Existence, penetrates all, and in fact He alone is the All. Ocean alone is all the waves; mud alone is all the mud-pots.

I have been a sinner due to lack of 'right knowledge' of Thy greatness, and so very much lived foolishly in the past. Therefore:

सखेति मत्वा प्रसभं यदुक्तं
हे कृष्ण हे यादव हे सखेति ।
अजानता महिमानं तवेदं
मया प्रमादात् प्रणयेन वापि ॥ ४१ ॥

Sakheti matvā prasabhaṁ yad-uktaṁ
he kṛṣṇa he yādava he sakheti,
ajānatā mahimānaṁ tavedaṁ
mayā pramādāt praṇayena vāpi.

सखा *sakhā* = friend; इति *iti* = as; मत्वा *matvā* = regarding; प्रसभम् *prasabham* = presumptuously; यत् *yat* = whatever; उक्तम् *uktam* = said; हे कृष्ण *he kṛṣṇa*= O *Kṛṣṇa*; हे यादव *he yādava* = O *Yādava*; हे सखा *he sakhā* = O friend; इति *iti* = thus; अजानता *ajānatā* = unknowing; महिमानम् *mahimānam* = greatness; तव *tava* = of yours; इदम् *idam* = this; मया *mayā* = by me; प्रमादात् *pramādāt* = from carelessness; प्रणयेन *praṇayena* = due to love; वा *vā* = or; अपि *api* = even.

41. *Whatever I have rashly said from carelessness or love, addressing You as "O* Kṛṣṇa, *O* Yādava, *O friend," and regarding You merely as a friend, unknowing of this greatness of Yours ...*

यच्चावहासार्थमसत्कृतोऽसि
विहारशय्यासनभोजनेषु ।
एकोऽथवाप्यच्युत तत्समक्षं
तत्क्षामये त्वामहमप्रमेयम् ॥ ४२ ॥

Yaccā-vahā-sārtha-masat-kṛto-'si
vihāra-śayyā-sana-bhojaneṣu,
eko-'thavā-pyacyuta tat-samakṣaṁ
tat-kṣāmaye tvā-mahama-prameyam.

यत् *yat* = whatever; च *ca* = and; अवहा-सार्थम् *avahā-sārtham* = for the sake of fun; असत् कृत: *asat kṛtaḥ* = dis-respectfully; असि *asi* = (thou) art; विहार-शय्या-आसन-भोजनेषु *vihāra-śayyā-āsana-bhojaneṣu* = while at play or on bed, while sitting or at meals; एक: *ekaḥ* = (when) one; अथवा *athavā* = or; अपि *api* = even; अच्युत *acyuta* = O *Acyuta*; तत् *tat* = so; समक्षम् *samaksam* = in company; तत् *tat* = that; क्षामये *kṣāmaye* = implore to forgive; त्वाम् *tvām* = you; अहम् *aham* = I; अप्रमेयम् *aprameyam* = immeasurable.

42. *In whatever way I may have insulted You for the sake of fun, while at play, reposing or sitting, or at meals, when alone (with You), O* Acyuta, *or in company—that, O Immeasurable One, I implore You to forgive.*

Here are two beautiful stanzas that bring to the forefront with dramatic precision, the exact type of emotions that will naturally be generated in any ordinary man, when he suddenly realises the Glory of the Divine. Even in our day-to-day life, a sudden realisation of the exact identity of a person to whom we have been so long talking, brings at once an apologetic tone in us. I had a chance to watch in a railway travel two businessmen talking to a third person about the irregularities and injustices of the Commerce Department in the country. Later on, after hours of free discussions, to the loving enquiries of the traders, the third man reluctantly had to admit that he was himself the Deputy Minister for Commerce in the then Government.

If you can now imagine the change in the faces of the blushing traders, you have rightly understood *Arjuna*'s emotions behind this stanza. Till now, *Arjuna* had thought Lord *Kṛṣṇa* to be nothing more than an intelligent cowherd boy, whom he had graciously patronised so long with his royal friendship. And with the realisation and recognition of *Kṛṣṇa*—the Infinite, the mortal in *Arjuna* prostrates in all loyalty and adoration and pleads for His Divine mercy and forgiveness.

There is a very intimate personal touch in these two stanzas wherein the philosophical discussions are tempered with the emotional touch of deep intimacy. The very effect of the *Gītā* is to bring the sonorous truths of the *Vedā-s* and the *Upaniṣad-s* to the happy tune of the work-a-day world. Great and thought-provoking *Vedāntik* truths have been suddenly brought down to the easy familiarity of a drawing-room-chat by such frequent psychological touches given by *Vyāsa*'s masterly pen. As an intimate friend, *Arjuna* must have, in rashness, not knowing *Kṛṣṇa*'s real Divine Nature, called Him familiarly by His pet names.

Again, in intimacy of his friendship, he must have addressed or expressed himself to *Kṛṣṇa* in some inappropriate bearings. For all these, *Arjuna* humbly asks Lord's forgiveness. These two stanzas together haul up to our gaze, the intense love that *Kṛṣṇa* and *Arjuna* had for each other. The *Arjuna-Kṛṣṇa* relationship could be likened to melodious poetry.

For........

पितासि लोकस्य चराचरस्य
त्वमस्य पूज्यश्च गुरुर्गरीयान् ।
न त्वत्समोऽस्त्यभ्यधिकः कुतोऽन्यो
लोकत्रयेऽप्यप्रतिमप्रभाव ॥ ४३ ॥

Pitāsi lokasya carā-carasya
tvamasya pūjyaś-ca gurur-garīyān,
na tvat-samo-'styabhya-dhikaḥ kuto-'nyo
loka-traye-'pya-pratima-prabhāva.

पिता *pītā* = father; असि *asi* = (you) are; लोकस्य *lokasya* = of the world; चर-अचरस्य *cara-acarasya* = of the moving and unmoving; त्वम् *tvam* = you; अस्य *asya* = of this; पूज्यः *pūjyaḥ* = to be revered; च *ca* = and; गुरुः *guruḥ* = the *Guru*; गरीयान् *garīyān* = weightier, greatest; न *na* = not; त्वत्-समः *tvat-samaḥ* = equal to you; अस्ति *asti* = is; अभ्यधिकः *abhyadhikaḥ* = superior, surpassing; कुतः *kutaḥ* = whence; अन्यः *anyaḥ* = other; लोक-त्रये *loka-traye* = in the three worlds; अपि *api* = also; अप्रतिम-प्रभाव *apratima-prabhāva* = O being of unequalled power.

43. *You are the Father of this world, moving and unmoving. You are to be adored by this world. You are the greatest* Guru, *(for) there exists none who is equal to You; how can there be then another, superior to You in the three worlds, O Being of unequalled power?*

Giving out his reasons for his utter surrender and for his entire loyalty to *Kṛṣṇa*, the Eternal Being, *Arjuna* sings this stanza. To consider the Lord of lords, as "the Father in Heaven," is not the prerogative of any particular religion, and if at all we find it anywhere, we can safely conclude, that either it is the instinctive expression of any prophet in expressing the relationship of the Truth with the false-world of names and forms, or that it is a direct borrowing from the *Hindū* scriptures*— the Mother of religions.

Here we find that *Arjuna*, bursting under the pressure of his voiceless emotion and his great regard for the Lord, addresses him: "*you are the father of the whole world (contituted of the) moving and unmoving.*" No doubt, the three worlds— consisting of our experiences in waking, dream, and deep-sleep states—are the interpretations of the same Eternal from the levels of the gross, the subtle and the causal bodies, and the Truth that illumines those experiences is everywhere one and the same.

Naturally, the Lord is, as Arjuna *says, "Of unequalled greatness," and there is none "superior to You in the three worlds." Because it is so:*

तस्मात्प्रणम्य प्रणिधाय कायं
प्रसादये त्वामहमीशमीड्यम् ।
पितेव पुत्रस्य सखेव सख्युः
प्रियः प्रियायार्हसि देव सोढुम् ॥ ४४ ॥

Tasmāt-praṇamya praṇidhāya kāyaṁ
prasādaye tvā-maha-mīśa-mīḍyam,
piteva putrasya sakheva sakhyuḥ
priyaḥ priyā-yārhasi deva soḍhum.

तस्मात् *tasmāt* = therefore; प्रणम्य *praṇamya* = saluting; प्रणिधाय *praṇidhāya* = having bent; कायम् *kāyam* = body; प्रसादये *prasādaye* = crave forgiveness; त्वाम् *tvām* = you; अहम् *aham* = I; ईशम् *īśam* = the Lord; ईड्यम् *īḍyam* = adorable; पिता *pitā* = father; इव *iva* = like; पुत्रस्य *putrasya* = of the son; सखा *sakhā* = friend; इव *iva* = like; सख्युः *sakhyuḥ* = of the friend; प्रियः *priyaḥ* = beloved; प्रियायाः

* *1. Ṛg Veda* says : "Be of easy approach to us, even as a father to his son, Be thou' O Self-effulgent Lord, abide with us and bring blessings to us.'

2. *Yajur Veda* says : "O Lord, you are the father, do instruct us like a father."

3. Bible says : "Like as a Father pitieth his children, so the Lord pitieth them that fear Him."

priyāyāḥ = to the beloved; अर्हसि *arhasi* = (you) should; देव *deva* = O God; सोढुम् *soḍhum* = bear, forgive (me).

44. *Therefore, bowing down, prostrating my body, I crave your forgiveness, O! adorable Lord. As a father for gives his son, a friend his friend, a lover his beloved, even so should You forgive me,* O Deva.

Arjuna seems to discover in himself a greater eloquence and a subtler ability to argue logically, with the realisation that he is in the presence of the Almighty, the Blessed. Prostration, in *Hindūism,* though generally practised as a physical act of touching-the-feet of the revered, is a significant act that is to be actually accomplished in our heart as a special inward attitude. Surrendering ourselves, so that we may rise above ourselves into the spiritual fields, is true prostration. The ego and ego-centric vagaries arising out of our false identifications with *matter* vestures have robbed us of our experience of the Divinity which is already in us. To the extent the mis-conceptions are annihilated, we, without these over-growths, are sure to realise the serener beauty of the Divine, which in reality, we are. In surrendering the ego unto the Lord, in fact, we have to bring to His feet nothing but a dirty bundle of animal *vāsanā-s*, putrified in our own stupidity and lust! Naturally, a devotee, reaching the feet of the Lord in a spirit of surrender and love, has to apologise for the filth that has been offered, as the only tribute of his love, at His Divine feet.

Arjuna is pleading here with the Lord to bear with him as "a father would with his son," as "a friend with his friend," as "a lover with his beloved." These three examples bring within their embrace all the types of immodest crimes that man, in his ignorance, can perpetrate against his Lord, the Creator.

Arjuna *now prays to the Lord to resume His usual form and give up the terrifying aspects of the transcendental and the universal:*

अदृष्टपूर्वं हृषितोऽस्मि दृष्ट्वा
भयेन च प्रव्यथितं मनो मे ।
तदेव मे दर्शय देव रूपं
प्रसीद देवेश जगन्निवास ॥ ४५ ॥

Adṛṣṭa-pūrvaṁ hṛṣito-'smi dṛṣṭvā
bhayena ca pravya-thitaṁ mano me,
tadeva me darśaya deva rūpaṁ
prasīda deveśa jagan-nivāsa.

अदृष्ट-पूर्वम् *adṛṣṭa-pūrvam* = what was never seen before; हृषित: *hṛṣitaḥ* = delighted; अस्मि *asmi* = (I) am; दृष्ट्वा *dṛṣṭvā* = having seen; भयेन *bhayena* = with fear; च *ca* = and; प्रव्यथितम् *pravyathitam* = is distressed; मन: *manaḥ* = mind; मे *me* = my; तत् *tat* = that; एव *eva* = only; मे *me* = to me; दर्शय *darśaya* = show; देव *deva* = O God; रूपम् *rūpam* = form; प्रसीद *prasīda* = have mercy; देव-ईश *deva-īśa* = O Lord of Gods; जगत्-निवास *jagat-nivāsa* = O abode of the Universe.

45. *I am delighted, having seen what was never seen before; and (yet) my mind is distressed with fear. Show me Your previous form only, O God; have mercy, O God of gods, O Abode of the Universe.*

Every devotee falls in love with the Lord of his devotion and thus when, from the *form* he gets transcended to the Infinite and Full nature of the *formless*, that was represented so long by the *form*, he experiences, no doubt, an Infinite Joy, but at that very moment he is overtaken by the emotion of "fear." This is the experience of every seeker during the days of his early attempts at getting over the evil of spiritual 'ignorance.' The new realm of joy lived within is, no doubt, absolutely blissful, but a sudden sense of fear exiles him back to body-consciousness and the consequent mental agitation.

At the dawn of his experience Divine, the limited ego, escaping all its limitations, enters into a world unknown to it so far, and it experiences with all joy the vastness of its own dynamism. *Arjuna* expresses his idea when he says, "*I am delighted, having seen what was never seen before.*" But in the earlier attempts, a seeker is not fit to maintain for long his equilibrium in that Divine Realm, and his mind seemingly dissolved to enter the *Still-moment-of-meditation*, revives again to flutter into activity, and we find, almost always, that it is the emotion of "fear" that the mind first experiences, when, with a dreadful shudder it crystallizes itself to sink into the welter of the body and its demands. At this time, a devotee identifies himself with his own emotions of love and devotion and implores the "Lord of his heart" to manifest His own sportive form of smiles and softness, of musical words and loving looks.

What exactly is the form in which Arjuna *wanted the Lord to appear before Him, is described in the following*:

किरीटिनं गदिनं चक्रहस्तम्
इच्छामि त्वां द्रष्टुमहं तथैव ।
तेनैव रूपेण चतुर्भुजेन
सहस्रबाहो भव विश्वमूर्ते ॥ ४६ ॥

Kirīṭinaṁ gadinaṁ cakra-hastam
icchāmi tvāṁ draṣṭu-mahaṁ tathaiva,
tenaiva rūpeṇa catur-bhujena
sahasra-bāho bhava viśva-mūrte.

किरीटिनम् *kiriṭinam* = crowned; गदिनम् *gadinam* = bearing a mace; चक्र-हस्तम् *cakra-hastam* = with a discus in the hand; इच्छामि *icchāmi* = (I) desire; त्वाम् *tvām* = you; द्रष्टुम् *draṣṭum* = to see; अहम् *aham* = I; तथा एव *tathā eva* = as before; तेन एव *tena eva* = that same; रूपेण *rūpeṇa* = of form; चतुर्भुजेन *catur-bhujena* = (by) four-armed; सहस्र-बाहो *sahasra-bāho* = O thousand-armed; भव *bhava* = be; विश्व-मूर्ते *viśva-mūrte* = universal form.

46. *I desire to see You as before, crowned, bearing a mace, with a discus in hand, in Your former*

form only, having four arms, O Thousand-armed, O Universal Form.

Arjuna makes an open confession here of what he actually wishes. "*I desire to see You as before.*" He is afraid of the Universal Form into which the Lord has expanded to express His oneness with the essence in the entire gross-world of *matter*.

When the *Vedāntik* concept of Truth is thus experienced or expressed in its universal majesty and grandeur, few have the required intellectual stamina to conceive of the Totality and adore It. Even at moments when the intellect can handle such an idea, the heart of the devotee will often fail to tune up its emotion to live the Absolute-experience for long. From the mental zone, Truth can be conceived of and enjoyed only through its symbols and not directly in Its Total-grandeur.

Defining the Form of *Vāsudeva* in his milder-manifestation, *Arjuna* explains in this stanza the traditional form of *Viṣṇu*, the Lord of the *Bhāgavata*. The concept of God as represented in the phenomena, has been described in all *Purāṇā-s*, as having four hands. This may look like a biological freak to the students of physiology. We are apt to forget that they are figurative representations symbolising the concept of Truth.

The four hands of the God-form represent the four facets of the "inner-instrument" in man.*

The Lord Himself, the Self who wields these four hands is represented everywhere as *blue* in colour, and clothed in *yellow*. The significant hue of *blue* is the colour of the Infinite, and the measureless always appears as *blue*, just as the summer-sky or the deep-ocean. *Yellow* is the colour of the earth. Thus the Infinite, clothed in the finite, playing the game of life through the four "inner-instruments" is the symbolism behind Lord *Viṣṇu*.

---

* Mind (*Manas*), intellect (*Buddhi*), thought-stuff (*Chitta*) and the ego-sense (*Ahaṅkāra*).

It is also interesting to note that the concept of God in every religion is the same inasmuch as He is the Supreme-most with every power and all knowledge. Man achieves things by the strength of His hands, and the Lord, who is all-powerful, can therefore be symbolised only by showing that He has four hands. The four symbolical instruments which the Lord is represented to carry in His four hands are the club, the discus, the conch and the lotus. The call of the Divine comes to everyone's bosom, when He blows His *conch*, and if man were not to listen to the call of the Higher dictates in himself, the *club* follows to punch him, and in spite of that, if man continues his own mistakes, the *discus* chops him down. In case the roar of the "conch" is obeyed implicitly, then he gains the *lotus*, a flower that represents, in *Hindūism*, what the white-dove and the poppy-flower stand for in Western tradition. Peace and prosperity are the significance of "lotus" in India. Lotus signifies *Perfection Spiritual*.

Arjuna, in short, wants the Lord to appear in his serener-Form and quieter-Attitude. For all early seekers and new initiates in *Vedānta*, it naturally becomes difficult to keep, in themselves, the same tempo for their philosophical pursuits. At such moments of dissipation and drowsiness of the intellect, the aspiring heart must discover some reposeful resting-place wherein it can revive itself. This bed-of-peace and tranquillity, upon which the inner personality of man can revive and grow into its fuller stature, is the glorious Form of the Lord.

Seeing Arjuna *afraid, the Lord withdrew his Universal Form, and consoling* Arjuna *with his sweet words, He said:*

श्रीभगवानुवाच–

मया प्रसन्नेन तवार्जुनेदं
रूपं परं दर्शितमात्मयोगात् ।
तेजोमयं विश्वमनन्तमाद्यं
यन्मे त्वदन्येन न दृष्टपूर्वम् ॥ ४७ ॥

Śrī Bhagavān Uvāca—

Mayā prasannena tavār-junedaṁ
rūpaṁ paraṁ darṣita-mātma-yogāt,
tejo-mayaṁ viśva-mananta-mādyaṁ
yanme tva-danyena na dṛṣṭa-pūrvam.

मया *mayā* = by me; प्रसन्नेन *prasannena* = gracious; तव *tava* = to you; अर्जुन *Arjuna* = O *Arjuna*; इदम् *idam* = this; रूपम् *rūpam* = form; परम् *param* = Supreme; दर्शितम् *darṣitam* = has been shown; आत्म-योगात् *ātma-yogāt* = by My own *Yoga* power; तेजोमयम् *tejo-mayam* = full of splendour; विश्वम् *viśvam* = universal; अनन्तम् *anantam* = endless; आद्यम् *ādyam* = primeval; यत् *yat* = which; मे *me* = of Me; त्वत् *tvat* = from you; अन्येन *anyena* = by another; न *na* = not; दृष्ट-पूर्वम् *dṛṣṭa-pūrvam* = seen before.

The Blessed Lord said:

47. *Graciously by Me, O* Arjuna, *this Supreme Form has been shown to you by My own* Yoga-*power—Full of splendour, Primeval, Infinite, this Universal Form of Mine has never been seen by any other than yourself.*

Here we have the confession that it is not the privilege of all devotees to come to perceive this "Form-tremendous" and that *Arjuna* is enjoying It as a special favour due to His Infinite Grace. He also asserts that, "Full of splendour, primeval, infinite, this universal form of mine has never been seen by any other than yourself."

It does not mean that *Vyāsa*, the author of the *Gītā*, is propounding a new theory, and is making the Lord of his own creation testify to the veracity of it. It only means that this intellectual realisation of the Universal-Oneness has not been gained by anyone placed in the same circumstances as those of *Arjuna* in the war-front. Mentally shattered, physically worn-out, emotionally upset—the miserable condition of *Arjuna* and this *Arjuna*-state of utter despondency are, in fact, far removed from the favourable conditions for a single-pointed intellectual quest, without which the underlying Principle of Oneness in the multiplicity of the gross world, cannot easily be comprehended. But *Kṛṣṇa* had, due to his tremendous powers, given the required 'eye-of-wisdom' to *Arjuna* and made him realise, in a chance moment of mental pause, the vision of the Cosmic Form.

What was at the back of the mind of the Lord, when he expressed this stanza, is clear from the following:

न वेदयज्ञाध्ययनैर्न दानैः
न च क्रियाभिर्न तपोभिरुग्रैः ।
एवंरूपः शक्य अहं नृलोके
द्रष्टुं त्वदन्येन कुरुप्रवीर ॥ ४८ ॥

Na veda-yajñā-dhyayanair-na dānaiḥ
na ca kriyābhir-na tapobhir-ugraiḥ,
evaṁ-rūpaḥ śakya ahaṁ nṛloke
draṣṭuṁ tva-danyena kuru-pravīra.

न *na* = not; वेद-यज्ञ-अध्ययनैः *veda-yajña-adhyayanaiḥ* = by the study of the *vedā-s* and *yajñā-s*; न *na* = not; दानैः *dānaiḥ*= by gifts; न *na* = not; च *ca* = and; क्रियाभिः *kriyābhiḥ* = by rituals; न *na* = not; तपोभिः *tapobhiḥ* = by austerities; उग्रैः *ugraiḥ* = severe; एवम्-रूपः *evam-rūpaḥ* = in such form; शक्य *śakya* = (am) possible; अहम् *aham* = I; नृलोके *nṛloke* = in the world of men; द्रष्टुम् *draṣṭum* = to be seen; त्वत् *tvat* = than yourself; अन्येन *anyena* = by another; कुरु-प्रवीर *kuru-pravīra* = O great hero of the *Kurū-s*.

48. *Neither by the study of the* Vedā-s *nor by sacrifices* (Yajñā-s), *nor by gifts, nor by rituals, nor by severe austerities, can I be seen in this form in the world of men by any other than yourself, O great hero among the Kurū-s.*

Explaining why *Arjuna* deserves a special congratulation for having gained this extraordinary experience, the Lord says that none can '*See*' this Universal-Form merely because of one's study of the *Vedā-s*, or on the strength of one's sacrifices. Nor can one gain it by the merits gained through the distribution of gifts, or through performing rituals, or even through constant practice of severe austerities. These are, no doubt, necessary and always helpful in preparing the seeker to realise the essential unity beneath the perceived plurality, but neither a mere book-study, nor empty ritualism, nor physical *tapas* in themselves will, as an effect of them, bring about this understanding and the Final Experience. It can come only when the mind is steady. This "Vision" can be illumined only in the clear light of an integrated 'in-turned intellect.'

In thus making light of the study of the *Vedā-s*, performance of sacrifices, distribution of gifts, practice of rituals and a life of grim penance, Lord *Kṛṣṇa* should not be misunderstood as ridiculing these great prescriptions of the *Vedā-s*. He merely means to say that although these are means, preparatory to the final end, they are not to be confused with the goal. Cooking, in itself, cannot appease hunger, but that does not mean that cooking is unnecessary; after cooking there is, and must be, the eating. It is in this sense that we must understand the stanza, criticising ponderous study and futile efforts of misguided enthusiasts.

For, none of the known methods of self-development is capable of producing this glorious achievement. It is said:

मा ते व्यथा मा च विमूढभावो
दृष्ट्वा रूपं घोरमीदृङ्ममेदम्‌ ।
व्यपेतभीः प्रीतमनाः पुनस्त्वं
तदेव मे रूपमिदं प्रपश्य ॥ ४९ ॥

Mā te vyathā mā ca vimūḍha-bhāvo
dṛṣṭvā rūpaṁ ghora-mīdṛṅma-medam,
vyapeta-bhīḥ prīta-manāḥ punas-tvaṁ
tadeva me rūpa-midaṁ prapaśya.

मा *mā* = not; ते *te* = thee; व्यथा *vyathā* = fear; मा *mā* = not; च *ca* = and; विमूढभाव: *vimūḍha-bhāvaḥ* = bewildered state; दृष्ट्वा *dṛṣṭvā* = having seen; रूपम् *rūpam* = form; घोरम् *ghoram* = terrible; ईदृक् *īdṛk* = such; मम *mama* = my; इदम् *idam* = this; व्यपेतभी: *vyapetabhīḥ* = with (thy) fear dispelled; प्रीत-मना: *prīta-manāḥ* = with gladdened heart; पुन: *punaḥ* = again; त्वम् *tvam* = thou; तत् *tat* = that; एव *eva* = even; मे *me* = my; रूपम् *rūpam* = form; इदम् *idam* = this;प्रपश्य *prapaśya* = behold.

49. *Be not afraid, nor bewildered on seeing such a terrible-form of Mine as this; with your fear dispelled and with gladdened heart, now behold again this (former) form of Mine.*

Vyāsa's dramatic genius will not fail to seek its fulfilment whenever an occasion arises. Here is an artistic example of such fine brush-work, accomplished by *Vyāsa* with words, on the canvas of the *Gītā*. *Arjuna*'s emotional agitations are dramatically indicated here when the Lord says, "*be not afraid, nor dewildered, having seen such a terrible-form of Mine.*"

Kṛṣṇa consoles his friend *Arjuna* by words and actions and helps him to be in a state of reassuring joys. The Lord comes back to His original form and announces His entry into it with the words: "*Now behold again this (former) form of Mine.*"

This passage, which announces the return of the Lord into His "gentler attitude" and "loving form," should remind all *Vedāntik* students of at least one of the great *Mahāvākyā-s.** The identity between the Universal-Form, the Terrible-Totality and the gentle Form-of-*Kṛṣṇa*, the Divine-individual, is

* *Tat Tvam Asi* or *Aham Brahma asmi* or *Ayam Ātma Brahma.*

beautifully brought about by the term *"this (former) form of Mine."** In fact, the micro-cosmic representation of Truth smiling temporarily from an assumed mortal-form of *Kṛṣṇa*, is Itself the macro-cosmic Universal-Form, wherein He expresses Himself as the Essence in all forms and names. The wave is in essence, the ocean; and if the ocean is mighty and fierce, terrible and gigantic, the wave itself is tame and bashful, lovable and attractive.

The scene again shifts from Kuruksetra *and the war-front to the quiet chambers of the luxurious palace in* Hastināpura, *where the blind old* Dhṛtarāstra *is listening to the running commentary given by his minister,* Sañjaya:

सञ्जय उवाच --

इत्यर्जुनं वासुदेवस्तथोक्त्वा
स्वकं रूपं दर्शयामास भूयः ।
आश्वासयामास च भीतमेनं
भूत्वा पुनः सौम्यवपुर्महात्मा ॥ ५० ॥

Sañjaya Uvāca—

Ityarjunaṁ vāsudevas-tathoktvā
svakaṁ rūpaṁ darśayā-māsa bhūyaḥ,
āśvāsayā-māsa ca bhīta-menaṁ
bhūtvā punaḥ saumya-vapur-mahātmā.

इति *iti* = thus; अर्जुनम् *Arjunaṁ* = to *Arjuna*; वासुदेवः *vāsudevaḥ* = son of *Vasudeva*; तथा *tathā* = so; उक्त्वा *uktvā* = having spoken; स्वकम् *svakam* = His own; रूपम् *rūpam* = form; दर्शयामास *darśayāmāsa* = showed; भूयः *bhūyaḥ* = again; आश्वासयामास *āśvāsayāmāsa* = consoled; च *ca* = and; भीतम् *bhītam* = who was terrified; एनम् *enam* = him; भूत्वा *bhūtvā* = having become;

---

* *"Tadeva Me Rūpam Idam."*

पुनः *punaḥ* = again; सौम्यवपुः *saumya-vapuḥ* = of gentle form; महात्मा *mahātmā* = the great-souled One.

Sañjaya said:

50. Having thus spoken to Arjuna, Vāsudeva *again showed His own form, and, the Great-souled One, assuming His gentle form, consoled him who was so terrified.*

Sañjaya confirms here to the blind old king that the terrible Universal-Form, after announcing Its intentions of coming back again to its original sweet form had actually accomplished that promise. What form *Kṛṣṇa* re-entered is evident: "*The very form in which He was born in the house of Vasudeva.*"* He assumed the pleasant shape of Lord *Kṛṣṇa*, the familiar friend of *Arjuna*, the Blue-Boy of the *Gopikā-s*, and thus consoled the mighty warrior, who was aghast with wonder, and trembling with "fear."

In these words of *Sañjaya*, we also can notice the minister's anxiety that Emperor *Dhṛtarāṣtra* should see the suggestion that the Lord of the Universe is *Kṛṣṇa*, and that *Kṛṣṇa* is on the side of the *Pāṇḍavā*-s. But how ... how will a blind man ever see?

The scene again shifts to the war-front when Sañjaya *reports the words of* Arjuna *in the following stanza:*

अर्जुन उवाच–

दृष्ट्वेदं मानुषं रूपं तव सौम्यं जनार्दन ।
इदानीमस्मि संवृत्तः सचेताः प्रकृतिं गतः ॥ ५१ ॥

Arjuna Uvāca—

Dṛṣṭvedaṁ mānuṣaṁ rūpaṁ tava saumyaṁ janārdana,
idānīm-asmi saṁvṛttaḥ sacetāḥ prakṛtiṁ gataḥ.

* *'Vasudeva gṛhe jatam rūpam'— Śaṅkara.*

दृष्ट्वा *dṛṣṭvā* = having seen; इदम् *idam* = this; मानुषम् *mānuṣam* = human; रूपम् *rūpam* = form; तव *tava* = thy; सौम्यम् *saumyam* = gentle; जनार्दन *janārdana* = O *Janārdana*; इदानीम् *idānīm* = now; अस्मि *asmi* = (I) am; संवृत्तः *saṁvṛttaḥ* = composed; सचेताः *sacetāḥ* = with mind; प्रकृतिम् *prakṛtim* = to nature; गतः *gataḥ* = restored.

Arjuna said:

51. *Having seen this, Thy gentle human-form,* O Janārdana, *I am now composed and restored to my own nature.*

Arjuna admits here that, when he sees the normal and the gentle-form of Lord *Kṛṣṇa*, he feels relieved from his inner tensions and agitations. When an unprepared student like *Arjuna* is suddenly pushed forward on the spiritual ladder and made to experience truths that are transcendental, and too vast for his intellectual comprehension, it is natural that even in that Realm-of-Bliss, he feels giddy confusions and heaving sobs. *Arjuna* admits: "I have now become collected in mind and am restored to my normal nature, having seen the milder aspect of *Kṛṣṇa*'s gracious human form."

True devotion to the universal form is explained hereunder:

श्रीभगवानुवाच-

सुदुर्दर्शमिदं रूपं दृष्टवानसि यन्मम ।
देवा अप्यस्य रूपस्य नित्यं दर्शनकांङ्क्षिणः ॥ ५२ ॥

Śrī Bhagavān Uvāca—

Sudur-darśam-idaṁ rūpaṁ dṛṣṭavā-nasi yan-mama,
devā apyasya rūpasya nityaṁ darśana-kāṅkṣiṇaḥ.

सुदुर्दर्शम् *sudur-darśam* = very hard to see; इदम् *idam* = this; रूपम् *rūpam* = form; दृष्टवानसि *dṛṣṭavānasi* = you have seen; यत् *yat* = which; मम *mama* = my; देवाः *devāḥ* = gods; अपि *api* = also; अस्य

asya = (of) this; रूपस्य *rūpasya* = of form; नित्यम् *nityam* = ever; दर्शन कांङ्क्षिण: *darśana-kāṅkṣiṇaḥ* = (are) desirous to behold.

The Blessed Lord said:

52. *Very hard, indeed, it is to see this form of Mine which you have seen. Even the gods are ever longing to behold this form.*

नाहं वेदैर्न तपसा न दानेन न चेज्यया ।
शक्य एवंविधो द्रष्टुं दृष्टवानसि मां यथा ॥ ५३ ॥

Nahaṁ vedair-na tapasā na dānena na cejyayā,
śakya evaṁ-vidho draṣṭuṁ dṛṣṭavā-nasi māṁ yathā.

न *na* = not; अहम् *aham* = I; वेदै: *vedaiḥ* = by the *Vedā-s*; न *na* = not; तपसा *tapasā* = by austerity; न *na* = not; दानेन *dānena* = by gift; न *na* = not; च *ca* = and; इज्यया *ijyayā* = by sacrifice i.e., *yajña*; शक्य *śakya* = (am) possible; एवंविध: *evaṁ-vidhaḥ* = like this; द्रष्टुम् *draṣṭum* = to be seen; दृष्टवानसि *dṛṣṭavānasi* = (you) have seen; माम् *mām* = me; यथा *yathā* = as.

53. *Neither by the* Vedā-s, *nor by austerity, nor by gift, nor by sacrifices can I be seen in this form as you have seen Me (in your present mental condition).*

The Universal-Form of the Lord is no easy experience for anyone, and it can be gained neither by study of the *Vedā-s*, nor by austerities, nor by gifts, nor by a sacrifice. Even the gods, the denizens of heaven, with their ampler intellects, longer lives, and harder endeavours, are unable to behold this Universal-Form, and they keep on longing for this experience.

And yet, *Kṛṣṇa* has shown this Form, mighty and wondrous, to His friend through His Grace, as He Himself admitted earlier.*

---

* XI-47: 'Through My grace this Supreme Form has been shown to you.'

We may wonder what makes the Lord shower His grace upon one, and not upon another. It cannot be a haphazard distribution of an Omnipotent, who does things as He likes, arbitrarily, without any rhyme or reason! For, in that case the Lord will be accused of partiality and arbitrariness.

The beauty in *Saṁskṛta* words in general and the mastery of *Vyāsa* at his pen in particular, can both be seen here in this stanza in the one simple word *Sudurdarśam.* This word is composed of *Su* plus *Du* plus *Darśam,* wherein *Su* stands for 'auspiciousness', *Du* for 'difficult', and *Darśa* for 'Sight.' Altogether it means that the vision of the Total Cosmic Form of the Lord is, no doubt, supremely auspicious, but at the same time it is extremely difficult to gain. With regard to the meaning pregnant in its words, no other language can ever come anywhere near the perfection met with in *Saṁskṛta.*

Here, in the following stanza, we get the scientific explanation of what compels the Lord to shower his special favours upon someone sometimes, and not upon all at all times:

भक्त्या त्वनन्यया शक्य अहमेवंविधोऽर्जुन ।
ज्ञातुं द्रष्टुं च तत्त्वेन प्रवेष्टुं च परंतप ॥ ५४ ॥

Bhaktyā tvana-nyayā śakya aham-evaṁ-vidho-'rjuna,
jñātuṁ draṣṭuṁ ca tattvena praveṣṭuṁ ca paraṁtapa.

भक्त्या *bhaktyā* = by devotion; तु *tu* = indeed; अनन्यया *ananyayā* = single-minded; शक्य *śakya* = (am) possible; अहम् *aham* = I; एवंविधः *evaṁvidhaḥ* = of this form; अर्जुन *Arjuna* = O *Arjuna*; ज्ञातुम् *jñātum* = to be known; द्रष्टुम् *draṣṭum* = to be seen; च *ca* = and; तत्त्वेन *tattvena* = in reality; प्रवेष्टुम् *praveṣṭum* = to be entered into; च *ca* = and; परंतप *paraṁtapa* = O *Paraṁtapa* (O Scorcher of foes).

54. *But, by single-minded devotion, can I, of this form, be 'known' and 'seen' in reality, and also 'entered' into,* O Paraṁtapa *(O scorcher of your foes)!*

This stanza explains why *Kṛṣṇa* has shown this real form to *Arjuna* which he had not shown to anyone else, and which is according to the Lord very difficult to gain. By undivided devotion alone can the Lord be experienced in the totality of the world of objects. Here the term devotion (*Bhakti*) should not be, in our haste, understood in its usual available meaning. Terms have a knack of gathering new implications and especially that of a living language, as also suffer from wear and tear because of indiscriminate and prolific use.

The term '*Bhakti*' had suffered both ways. In has been stripped off its deeper implications and has gathered a host of superstitious formalities in its embrace.

Regarding devotion *Śaṅkara* says*: "No doubt, of the means available for liberating ourselves, the most substantial hardware is *Bhakti*; and identifying ourselves with the Self is called *Bhakti*."

Identification is the truest measure of Love. The devotee, forgetting his own individual existence and, in his love, identifying to become one with his beloved Lord, is the culmination of Divine Love. The *Vedāntik* student who is the seeker of the Self, is spiritually obliged to renounce all his abject identification with his *matter*-vestures and to discover his true nature to be the Self.

Only those who are thus capable of identifying themselves with the One unifying Truth that holds together, in its web-of-love, the plurality, can experience, "*Me in this fashion*"—in my Cosmic Form.

The three stages in which realisation of Truth comes to man are indicated here when the Lord says, "*to know, to see, and to enter*." A definite intellectual knowledge of the goal and the path is the beginning of a seeker's pilgrimage—*To know*. Next comes the seeker's attempt to masticate the ideas

---

* Refer *Svāmījī's* commentary on *Vivekacūḍāmaṇi*—stanza 31.

intellectually understood through his own personal reflections upon the information which he has already gathered—*To see.* Having thus 'known' and 'seen' the goal, thereafter, the seeker, through a process of detachment from the false and attachment to the Real, comes to experience the Truth as no object other than himself—*To enter.* By the term 'entering,' it is also indicated that the fulfilled seeker becomes the very essence of the sought. The dreamer, suffering from the sorrows of the dream, ends it all, when he no more sees, but "enters" the waking-state, himself to become the waker.

How? ... I shall explain, says the Lord and adds:

मत्कर्मकृन्मत्परमो मद्भक्तः सङ्गवर्जितः ।
निर्वैरः सर्वभूतेषु यः स मामेति पाण्डव ॥ ५५ ॥

Matkarma-kṛn-matparamo mad-bhaktaḥ saṅga-varjitaḥ,
nir-vairaḥ sarva-bhūteṣu yaḥ sa māmeti pāṇḍava.

मत्कर्मकृत् *mat-karma-kṛt* = does actions for me; मत्परमः *mat-paramaḥ* = looks on me as the Supreme; मद्भक्तः *mad-bhaktaḥ* = is devoted to me; सङ्गवर्जितः *saṅga-varjitaḥ* = is freed from attachment; निर्वैरः *nir-vairaḥ* = without enmity; सर्व-भूतेषु *sarva-bhūteṣu* = towards all creatures; यः *yaḥ* = who; सः *saḥ* = he; माम् *mām* = to me; एति *eti* = goes, comes, attains; पाण्डव *pāṇḍava* = O *Pāṇḍava.*

55. *He who does actions for Me, who looks upon Me as the Supreme, who is devoted to Me, who is free from attachment, who bears enmity (hatred) towards none, he comes to Me,* O Pāṇḍava.

When he heard that anyone can, through undivided devotion, not only recognise the cosmic might of the Lord but also experience that glory in himself, the *Pāṇḍava* Prince's face must have reflected an anxiety to acquire this status. As an answer to this unasked question from *Arjuna*, *Kṛṣṇa* explains here how one can grow towards this great fulfilment in life.

The *Kṛṣṇa*-plan, for finite man to gain the stature and strength of the Cosmic, seems to consist of five distinct schemes. This is clear from the conditions required of a seeker as given in this verse. They are:

(1) Whose work is all dedicated to the Lord,

(2) Whose goal is the Lord,

(3) Who is a devotee of the Lord,

(4) Who is free from all attachments, and

(5) Who is devoid of all sense of enmity (hatred) towards everyone.

In these five schemes, we find the entire line of self-discipline summarised. Detachment from all activities, whether physical or mental or intellectual can take place only when one is constantly thinking of the Self. Enmity is possible only when one considers the others as separate from oneself. There cannot be enmity between my own right hand and my left hand. The awareness of the Oneness should be experienced through the vision of the same Self everywhere and then alone can the total avoidance of enmity with any creature be fully accomplished.

Total detachment is an impossibility at the mind-and-intellect level. The mind and intellect cannot live without attaching themselves to some thing or being. Therefore, the seeker, through God-dedicated activity, learns first to withdraw all his attachments from other things, and then to turn his mind with the fervour of devoted attachment to the Lord. In accomplishing this, all the schemes explained earlier are, indeed, very helpful.

Thus, when the whole scheme is re-evaluated, we can find in it a logic quite acceptable and perfectly psychological. Each subsequent item in the scheme is beautifully supported and nourished by the previous one. From the stanza, it is evident that the spiritual seeker's great pilgrimage starts with God-dedicated activities. Soon, that God-principle Itself becomes his very goal in life. He will develop, in himself, a consummate liking for this glorious goal. Naturally, all his other finite attachments with the world-of-objects will end, and at last, he will come to contact the Self. Having become the Self, he recognises himself everywhere, in everything, and so, in him there cannot be any sense of enmity at all.

Love for all and hatred for none can be considered the *Gītā* 'touch-stone' to know the quality of realisation and intensity of experience a seeker has gained through his *Sādhanā*.

ॐ तत्सदिति श्रीमद् भगवद् गीतासु उपनिषत्सु
ब्रह्मविद्यायां योगशास्त्रे श्रीकृष्णार्जुन संवादे
'विश्वरूपदर्शनयोगो' नाम
एकादशोऽध्यायः ॥ ११ ॥

Oṁ tat-sat-iti Śrīmad-Bhagavad-Gītāsu Upaniṣatsu
brahma-vidyāyāṁ yoga-śāstre Śrī Kṛṣṇārjuna saṁvāde
'viśva-rūpa-darśana-yogo' nāma
ekādaśo-'dhyāyaḥ.

Thus, in the *Upaniṣad-s* of the glorious *Bhagavad Gītā*, in the Science of the Eternal, in the scripture of *Yoga*, in the dialogue between *Śrī Kṛṣṇa* and *Arjuna*, the fifth discourse ends entitled:

THE YOGA OF THE VISION OF
THE UNIVERSAL FORM

The Chapter is rightly named as the *Vision of the Universal-Form*. In *Saṁskṛta* scriptural terminology, it is pointed out that the term *Viśva-rūpa* used here is actually the *Virāṭ-rūpa*. The Self, identifying itself with an 'individual physical body,' experiences the waking-state happenings, and in this condition the Self is called in *Vedānta* as *Viśva*. When the same Self identifies Itself with the total-physical-gross-bodies of the Universe, in that condition the Self is called the

Cosmic—*Virāṭ*. Here the Lord showed His Cosmic-Form but the Chapter is titled as *Viśva-rūpa*.

This can be justified in two ways. The *Ācārya,* who has supplied us with these epilogues, generally attributed to *Madhusūdan Sarasvatī*, the great commentator of the *Mahābhārata,* wants to convey to the ordinary reader the Cosmic Form by the familiar term, suggestive in itself to the Indian students, *Viśva-rūpa.* Again *Viśva*, as a term in itself, is used in our literature to indicate the total world of experiences that all beings live through, at all times either through their physical or mental or intellectual medium, it is very appropriate to name the chapter as *Viśva-rūpa Darśana* to mean vision of the "Total Cosmic Form."

For the rest of the terms in the *Saṅkalpa Vākya*, please refer to the exhaustive notes given at the end of Chapters I II and III.

Oṁ Oṁ Oṁ

Ślokā-s

अर्जुन उवाच-

मदनुग्रहाय परमं गुह्यमध्यात्मसंज्ञितम् ।
यत्त्वयोक्तं वचस्तेन मोहोऽयं विगतो मम ॥ १ ॥

भवाप्ययौ हि भूतानां श्रुतौ विस्तरशो मया ।
त्वत्तः कमलपत्राक्ष माहात्म्यमपि चाव्ययम् ॥ २ ॥

एवमेतद्यथात्थ त्वमात्मानं परमेश्वर ।
द्रष्टुमिच्छामि ते रूपमैश्वरं पुरुषोत्तम ॥ ३ ॥

मन्यसे यदि तच्छक्यं मया द्रष्टुमिति प्रभो ।
योगेश्वर ततो मे त्वं दर्शयात्मानमव्ययम् ॥ ४ ॥

श्रीभगवानुवाच-

पश्य मे पार्थ रूपाणि शतशोऽथ सहस्रशः ।
नानाविधानि दिव्यानि नानावर्णाकृतीनि च ॥ ५ ॥

पश्यादित्यान्वसून्रुद्रानश्विनौ मरुतस्तथा ।
बहून्यदृष्टपूर्वाणि पश्याश्चर्याणि भारत ॥ ६ ॥

इहैकस्थं जगत्कृत्स्नं पश्याद्य सचराचरम् ।
मम देहे गुडाकेश यच्चान्यद् द्रष्टुमिच्छसि ॥ ७ ॥

न तु मां शक्यसे द्रष्टुमनेनैव स्वचक्षुषा ।
दिव्यं ददामि ते चक्षुः पश्य मे योगमैश्वरम् ॥ ८ ॥

सञ्जय उवाच-

एवमुक्त्वा ततो राजन्महायोगेश्वरो हरिः ।
दर्शयामास पार्थाय परमं रूपमैश्वरम् ॥ ९ ॥

अनेकवक्त्रनयनमनेकाद्भुतदर्शनम् ।
अनेकदिव्याभरणं दिव्यानेकोद्यतायुधम् ॥ १० ॥

दिव्यमाल्याम्बरधरं दिव्यगन्धानुलेपनम् ।
सर्वाश्चर्यमयं देवमनन्तं विश्वतोमुखम् ॥ ११ ॥

दिवि सूर्यसहस्रस्य भवेद्युगपदुत्थिता ।
यदि भाः सदृशी सा स्याद्भासस्तस्य महात्मनः ॥ १२ ॥

तत्रैकस्थं जगत्कृत्स्नं प्रविभक्तमनेकधा ।
अपश्यद् देवदेवस्य शरीरे पाण्डवस्तदा ॥ १३ ॥

ततः स विस्मयाविष्टो हृष्टरोमा धनञ्जयः ।
प्रणम्य शिरसा देवं कृताञ्जलिरभाषत ॥ १४ ॥

अर्जुन उवाच-

पश्यामि देवांस्तव देव देहे सर्वांस्तथा भूतविशेषसंघान् ।
ब्रह्माणमीशं कमलासनस्थम् ऋषींश्च सर्वानुरगांश्च दिव्यान् ॥१५॥

अनेकबाहूदरवक्त्रनेत्रं पश्यामि त्वां सर्वतोऽनन्तरूपम् ।
नान्तं न मध्यं न पुनस्तवादिं पश्यामि विश्वेश्वर विश्वरूप ॥१६॥

किरीटिनं गदिनं चक्रिणं च तेजोराशिं सर्वतो दीप्तिमन्तम् ।
पश्यामि त्वां दुर्निरीक्ष्यं समन्तात् दीप्तानलार्कद्युतिमप्रमेयम् ॥१७॥

त्वमक्षरं परमं वेदितव्यं त्वमस्य विश्वस्य परं निधानम् ।
त्वमव्ययः शाश्वतधर्मगोप्ता सनातनस्त्वं पुरुषो मतो मे ॥ १८॥

अनादिमध्यान्तमनन्तवीर्यम् अनन्तबाहुं शशिसूर्यनेत्रम् ।
पश्यामि त्वां दीप्तहुताशवक्त्रं स्वतेजसा विश्वमिदं तपन्तम् ॥१९॥

द्यावापृथिव्योरिदमन्तरं हि व्याप्तं त्वयैकेन दिशश्च सर्वाः ।
दृष्ट्वाद्भुतं रूपमुग्रं तवेदं लोकत्रयं प्रव्यथितं महात्मन् ॥ २० ॥

अमी हि त्वां सुरसंघा विशन्ति के
चिद्भीताः प्राञ्जलयो गृणन्ति ।
स्वस्तीत्युक्त्वा महर्षिसिद्धसंघाः
स्तुवन्ति त्वां स्तुतिभिः पुष्कलाभिः ॥ २१ ॥

रुद्रादित्या वसवो ये च साध्या विश्वेऽश्विनौ मरुतश्चोष्मपाश्च ।
गन्धर्वयक्षासुर सिद्धसंघा वीक्षन्ते त्वां विस्मिताश्चैव सर्वे ॥ २२ ॥

रूपं महत्ते बहुवक्त्रनेत्रं महाबाहो बहुबाहूरुपादम् ।
बहूदरं बहुदंष्ट्राकरालं दृष्ट्वा लोकाः प्रव्यथितास्तथाहम् ॥ २३ ॥

नभःस्पृशं दीप्तमनेकवर्णं
व्यात्ताननं दीप्तविशालनेत्रम् ।
दृष्ट्वा हि त्वां प्रव्यथितान्तरात्मा
धृतिं न विन्दामि शमं च विष्णो ॥ २४ ॥

दंष्ट्राकरालानि च ते मुखानि दृष्ट्वैव कालानलसन्निभानि ।
दिशो न जाने न लभे च शर्म प्रसीद देवेश जगन्निवास ॥ २५ ॥

अमी च त्वां धृतराष्ट्रस्य पुत्राः सर्वे सहैवावनिपालसंघैः।
भीष्मो द्रोणः सूतपुत्रस्तथासौ सहास्मदीयैरपि योधमुख्यैः॥ २६ ॥

वक्त्राणि ते त्वरमाणा विशन्ति दंष्ट्राकरालानि भयानकानि ।
केचिद्विलग्ना दशनान्तरेषु संदृश्यन्ते चूर्णितैरुत्तमाङ्गैः॥ २७ ॥

यथा नदीनां बहवोऽम्बुवेगाः समुद्रमेवाभिमुखा द्रवन्ति ।
तथा तवामी नरलोकवीरा विशन्ति वक्त्राण्यभिविज्वलन्ति ॥२८॥

यथा प्रदीप्तं ज्वलनं पतङ्गा
विशन्ति नाशाय समृद्धवेगाः ।
तथैव नाशाय विशन्ति लोकाः
तवापि वक्त्राणि समृद्धवेगाः ॥ २९ ॥

लेलिह्यसे ग्रसमानः समन्तात् लोकान्समग्रान्वदनैर्ज्वलद्भिः ।
तेजोभिरापूर्य जगत्समग्रंभासस्तवोग्राः प्रतपन्ति विष्णो ॥ ३० ॥

आख्याहि मे को भवानुग्ररूपो नमोऽस्तु ते देववर प्रसीद ।
विज्ञातुमिच्छामि भवन्तमाद्यं न हि प्रजानामि तव प्रवृत्तिम् ॥ ३१ ॥

श्रीभगवानुवाच-

कालोऽस्मि लोकक्षयकृत्प्रवृद्धो
लोकान्समाहर्तुमिह प्रवृत्तः ।
ऋतेऽपि त्वां न भविष्यन्ति सर्वे
येऽवस्थिताः प्रत्यनीकेषु योधाः ॥ ३२ ॥

तस्मात्त्वमुत्तिष्ठ यशो लभस्व
जित्वा शत्रून् भुङ्क्ष्व राज्यं समृद्धम् ।
मयैवैते निहताः पूर्वमेव
निमित्तमात्रं भव सव्यसाचिन् ॥ ३३ ॥

द्रोणं च भीष्मं च जयद्रथं च
कर्णं तथान्यानपि योधवीरान् ।
मया हतांस्त्वं जहि मा व्यथिष्ठा
युध्यस्व जेतासि रणे सपत्नान् ॥ ३४ ॥

सञ्जय उवाच-

एतच्छ्रुत्वा वचनं केशवस्य कृताञ्जलिर्वेपमानः किरीटी ।
नमस्कृत्वा भूय एवाह कृष्णं सगद्गदं भीतभीतः प्रणम्य॥३५॥

अर्जुन उवाच-

स्थाने हृषीकेश तव प्रकीर्त्या जगत्प्रहृष्यत्यनुरज्यते च ।
रक्षांसि भीतानि दिशो द्रवन्ति सर्वे नमस्यन्ति च सिद्धसंघाः॥३६॥

कस्माच्च ते न नमेरन्महात्मन् गरीयसे ब्रह्मणोऽप्यादिकर्त्रे ।
अनन्त देवेश जगन्निवास त्वमक्षरं सदसत्तत्परं यत् ॥ ३७ ॥

त्वमादिदेवः पुरुषः पुराणः त्वमस्य विश्वस्य परं निधानम् ।
वेत्तासि वेद्यं च परं च धाम त्वया ततं विश्वमनन्तरूप ॥३८॥

वायुर्यमोऽग्निर्वरुणः शशाङ्कः प्रजापतिस्त्वं प्रपितामहश्च ।
नमो नमस्तेऽस्तु सहस्रकृत्वः पुनश्च भूयोऽपि नमो नमस्ते ॥३९॥

नमः पुरस्तादथ पृष्ठतस्ते नमोऽस्तु ते सर्वत एव सर्व ।
अनन्तवीर्यामितविक्रमस्त्वं सर्वं समाप्नोषि ततोऽसि सर्वः॥ ४० ॥

सखेति मत्वा प्रसभं यदुक्तं हे कृष्ण हे यादव हे सखेति ।
अजानता महिमानं तवेदं मया प्रमादात् प्रणयेन वापि ॥ ४१ ॥

यच्चावहासार्थमसत्कृतोऽसि विहारशय्यासनभोजनेषु ।
एकोऽथवाप्यच्युत तत्समक्षं तत्क्षामये त्वामहमप्रमेयम् ॥ ४२ ॥

पितासि लोकस्य चराचरस्य
त्वमस्य पूज्यश्च गुरुर्गरीयान् ।
न त्वत्समोऽस्त्यभ्यधिकः कुतोऽन्यो
लोकत्रयेऽप्यप्रतिमप्रभाव ॥ ४३ ॥

तस्मात्प्रणम्य प्रणिधाय कायं प्रसादये त्वामहमीशमीड्यम् ।
पितेव पुत्रस्य सखेव सख्युः प्रियः प्रियायार्हसि देव सोढुम्॥ ४४ ॥

अदृष्टपूर्वं हृषितोऽस्मि दृष्ट्वा भयेन च प्रव्यथितं मनो मे ।
तदेव मे दर्शय देव रूपं प्रसीद देवेश जगन्निवास ॥ ४५ ॥

किरीटिनं गदिनं चक्रहस्तम् इच्छामि त्वां द्रष्टुमहं तथैव ।
तेनैव रूपेण चतुर्भुजेन सहस्रबाहो भव विश्वमूर्ते ॥ ४६ ॥

श्रीभगवानुवाच–
मया प्रसन्नेन तवार्जुनेदं रूपं परं दर्शितमात्मयोगात् ।
तेजोमयं विश्वमनन्तमाद्यं यन्मे त्वदन्येन न दृष्टपूर्वम् ॥ ४७ ॥

न वेदयज्ञाध्ययनैर्न दानैः न च क्रियाभिर्न तपोभिरुग्रैः ।
एवंरूपः शक्य अहं नृलोके द्रष्टु त्वदन्येन कुरुप्रवीर ॥ ४८ ॥

मा ते व्यथा मा च विमूढभावो दृष्ट्वा रूपं घोरमीदृङ्ममेदम् ।
व्यपेतभीः प्रीतमनाः पुनस्त्वं तदेव मे रूपमिदं प्रपश्य ॥ ४९ ॥

सञ्जय उवाच --

इत्यर्जुनं वासुदेवस्तथोक्त्वा स्वकं रूपं दर्शयामास भूयः ।
आश्वासयामास च भीतमेनं भूत्वा पुनः सौम्यवपुर्महात्मा ॥ ५० ॥

अर्जुन उवाच-

दृष्ट्वेदं मानुषं रूपं तव सौम्यं जनार्दन ।
इदानीमस्मि संवृत्तः सचेताः प्रकृतिं गतः ॥ ५१ ॥

श्रीभगवानुवाच-

सुदुर्दर्शमिदं रूपं दृष्टवानसि यन्मम ।
देवा अप्यस्य रूपस्य नित्यं दर्शनकांङ्क्षिणः ॥ ५२ ॥

नाहं वेदैर्न तपसा न दानेन न चेज्यया ।
शक्य एवंविधो द्रष्टुं दृष्टवानसि मां यथा ॥ ५३ ॥

भक्त्या त्वनन्यया शक्य अहमेवंविधोऽर्जुन ।
ज्ञातुं द्रष्टुं च तत्त्वेन प्रवेष्टुं च परंतप ॥ ५४ ॥

मत्कर्मकृन्मत्परमो मद्भक्तः सङ्गवर्जितः ।
निर्वैरः सर्वभूतेषु यः स मामेति पाण्डव ॥ ५५ ॥

ॐ तत्सदिति श्रीमद् भगवद् गीतासु उपनिषत्सु
ब्रह्मविद्यायां योगशास्त्रे श्रीकृष्णार्जुन संवादे
'विश्वरूपदर्शनयोगो' नाम
एकादशोऽध्यायः ॥ ११ ॥